Empowering Young
Voices for the Planet

Empowering Young Voices for the Planet

Lynne Cherry

Juliana Texley

Suzanne Lyons

CORWIN
A SAGE Company

CORWIN
A SAGE Company

FOR INFORMATION:

Corwin
A SAGE Company
2455 Teller Road
Thousand Oaks, California 91320
(800) 233-9936
www.corwin.com

SAGE Publications Ltd.
1 Oliver's Yard
55 City Road
London EC1Y 1SP
United Kingdom

SAGE Publications India Pvt. Ltd.
B 1/I 1 Mohan Cooperative Industrial Area
Mathura Road, New Delhi 110 044
India

SAGE Publications Asia-Pacific Pte. Ltd.
3 Church Street
#10-04 Samsung Hub
Singapore 049483

For photo credits, see the *Young Voices for the Planet* films at http://www.youngvoicesonclimate change.com.

Printed in the United States of America

ISBN 9781483317236

Acquisitions Editor: Jessica Allan
Associate Editor: Kimberly Greenberg
Editorial Assistant: Cesar Reyes
Project Editor: Veronica Stapleton Hooper
Copy Editor: Judy Selhorst
Typesetter: C&M Digitals (P) Ltd.
Proofreader: Sarah J. Duffy
Indexer: Maria Sosnowski
Interior Designer: Scott Van Atta
Cover illustration: Lynne Cherry
Cover Logo and Design: Tom Lempner,
                       Radiant Design
Marketing Strategist: Maura Sullivan

This book is printed on acid-free paper

SUSTAINABLE FORESTRY INITIATIVE
Certified Chain of Custody
Promoting Sustainable Forestry
www.sfiprogram.org
SFI-01268

SFI label applies to text stock

14 15 16 17 18 10 9 8 7 6 5 4 3 2 1

Contents

Preface

This book is all about energy—the energy we produce, the energy we use, the energy we waste as we devastate our climate—and the energy of youth who hold the power to shape the future of Earth. *Empowering Young Voices for the Planet* supports an award-winning collection of films that document the power of young people to preserve our planet.

This book is also a guide to *energy management*. In it you'll find ways to use the incredibly energizing stories of youth in action in your classroom and community. You'll see what can be accomplished and learn how to empower more young voices. This is a manual to help mentors and guides. Prepare to be fired up!

The films in the *Young Voices for the Planet* collection describe the true stories of nine youth projects. Beginning with nothing but enthusiasm, young scientist-activists have accomplished amazing things. Some of these projects started with school enrichment groups, some with clubs, and some with Scouts. Other projects began with outstanding individuals— true leaders—who saw problems and imagined solutions. Many of them had influential mentors, but the credit is all theirs. Through the films and the activities on the pages that follow you can learn about their paths to success and be inspired to find your own.

The *Young Voices for the Planet* films have been well received by large audiences at the United Nations, the American Museum of Natural History in New York, the Denver Museum of Nature and Science, and the annual conferences of the Association of Science-Technology Centers (ASTC), the American Bar Association's Environmental Law Conference, and the National Science Teachers Association. The films were screened at COP15 (the international climate talks in Copenhagen) and included in the "prep kit" for Next Generation, a program that helps students in Copenhagen develop sustainable strategies for their schools and communities. The films also toured with the Mountainfilm in Telluride and Wild & Scenic traveling film festivals. Everywhere they go, the films are making an impact.

In the introduction to this teaching guide, you will learn about the *Young Voices for the Planet* approach to teaching climate change. As you'll see, we use an innovative pedagogical strategy incorporating several key findings from recent research as well as insights gained from the observed success of the *Young Voices* films. Our approach to climate change education is mindful of the psychological impact of alarming scientific information. Past approaches to climate change have engendered fear and denial by focusing too much on the disturbing truth about climate change and not enough on the positive actions students can take to prevent dread scenarios from occurring. The *Young Voices* program is pioneering a positive alternative that replaces fear-based instruction with action-oriented inspiration.

Part I of this teaching guide will help you build lesson plans based on the films. As you will see, we present a synopsis of each film along with classroom activities and literacy prompts to help you integrate the films into your curriculum. Part I also features correlations to the Next Generation Science Standards (NGSS) and Common Core for each section. Lessons for the films can fall naturally into almost any system's middle-level program with plenty of possible extensions into elementary school and high school curricula.

For example, the films and activities can be used as an introduction to climate science or to an energy curriculum for upper elementary through high school. Or they can be integrated into individual lessons on science, technology, engineering, or mathematics (STEM), social studies, or environmental studies. They can also be used to teach about democracy and civic engagement. Finally, you can *STEAM* up your classroom by infusing the arts-based activities in this guide into STEM curricula.

Part II of this book is a practical action guide to beginning a project that is important to your own community. Whether the project is integrated into the regular curriculum, structured for enrichment or remediation, or organized under the auspices of a club or community effort, you'll find many practical tips for success. "Think globally, act locally" isn't just a bumper sticker. It's the game plan for exciting and powerful student activism. Part II describes how in-school and after-school groups can begin their own efforts to save the planet from human harm. Here you'll find nitty-gritty details on planning, financing, safety, and liability.

We hope that you will use the films along with the Part II action guide to start a project in your own community of learners. We're confident that once you allow your students to open up their experience and imagination, they can take the lead. So you may want to let your students choose whether they would like to replicate one or more of the projects in the

Young Voices for the Planet films or develop their own projects for reducing carbon dioxide (CO_2) emissions. The possibilities are endless. You might set up a community screening of the films followed by a presentation of the students' CO_2-reduction projects. Or show the films to inspire members of the larger school community as to what might be possible. The films are great for theatrical as well as classroom screenings. Shown back-to-back all together or individually, they can be used as an introduction to your own action science efforts. Often, youth inspire their communities when they speak after screenings at film festivals—or at such venues as landmark movie theaters or local multiplexes—and share information about their science and service projects.

So don't hesitate to encourage such efforts in your school and community. Youth activism doesn't have to be highly political. Students don't need to take sides or associate themselves with a partisan movement. In the best tradition of a democratic society, students can look at different sides of an issue, do scientific research, work together, and use creative thinking to help solve serious environmental and societal problems.

The human journey to save the planet's fragile ecosystems has begun. Now is the time for your students to join the adventure!

About the Authors

Lynne Cherry M.A., is an author, illustrator, film-maker, and lecturer. She has written and illustrated thirty award-winning books for children, including her best sellers *The Great Kapok Tree* and *A River Ran Wild*. Lynne is also the producer and director of the *Young Voices for the Planet* movie series, which focuses on youth empowerment.

Lynne earned a B.A. at Tyler School of Art, a B.S. in education and teaching certificate from Temple University, and a master's degree in history at Yale University. She has had artist-in-residencies at Princeton University, the Smithsonian Institution, and Cornell University and science-writing fellowships from the Marine Biological Lab and Woods Hole Oceanographic Institution.

Lynne has been awarded a Metcalf Fellowship and the Brandwein Prize. She also writes for adults and, most recently, published a chapter in *Written in Water: Messages of Hope for Earth's Most Precious Resource*, edited by Irena Salina (2010).

Juliana Texley, Ph.D., has taught science at every level from PreK through graduate school for four decades. As a secondary science teacher, she was awarded a Presidential Award for Excellence in Mathematics and Science Teaching.

She was a school superintendent of a rapidly growing district for nine years, during which time she coordinated a series of building projects that won national awards. Her work as an administrator included a number of leadership positions in curriculum development in Michigan, including chairperson and lead editor of the state's SCOPE project for three years.

Juliana also served as editor of *The Science Teacher,* the National Science Teachers Association's secondary journal, for twelve years and as lead reviewer for science publications for the NSTA's Recommends online database for another twelve years. She has served on the boards of the National Science Foundation and Biological Sciences Curriculum Study, as well as chairing task forces for the NSTA. She has published six books for teachers and one book of historical fiction, as well as many peer-reviewed articles in journals.

She currently teaches biology, oceanography, environmental science, and technology for four colleges and universities. As a leader in the development of educational technology, she has written online curricula for National Geographic/JASON as well as programs for the National Oceanic and Atmospheric Administration, the National Institutes of Health, and the U.S. Department of Agriculture. In 2014–2015 she will serve as president of the National Science Teachers Association.

 Suzanne Lyons, M.A., M.A., is a science educator and author. Her works range from textbooks to fiction and nonfiction books for kids, teaching manuals, and online resources from tutorials to games. Suzanne likes science learning to be fun, personally meaningful, and socially relevant. To that end, she founded CooperativeGames.com, a supplier of cooperative games for education. Suzanne received a B.A. in physics from the University of California, Berkeley, an M.A. in Earth science from Cal State Sacramento, and an M.A. in science education and a California teaching credential from Stanford University.

Suzanne began her career in education at Lawrence Hall of Science at UC Berkeley, where she developed a learning resource center for the Chemical Education for Public Understanding Project (CEPUP) while still a student. She became staff scientist at a biophysics start-up company early on, but soon returned to her passion for science education. She has taught science at all levels K–12 and has lectured at the university level. She currently teaches Earth science and integrated science at ConceptualAcademy.com.

Suzanne coauthored *Conceptual Integrated Science,* a textbook program published in 2005. She coauthored the middle school version, *Conceptual Integrated Science—Explorations,* in 2009. Both programs are sold internationally.

Introduction

The Young Voices Approach to Teaching Climate Change

Educators, academicians, scientists, and the scientifically and environmentally aware public agree that it is essential for students to have an understanding of Earth systems and climate change science. Global climate change is upon us, and it will play a huge part in the future of youth worldwide.

But teaching about climate change has proven challenging because students often turn off and shut down when they begin to understand its dire consequences. Learning about climate change can easily engender fear leading to denial or apathy. It is often easier to deny the science than to embrace the reality of a planetary emergency.

So it is essential that we go beyond science content when teaching climate change. Thus this book pairs scientific content with the *Young Voices for the Planet* films. These films showcase stories of youth solutions to the climate crisis, providing real models of positive pathways to change. As Shannon McComb (age thirteen) says in one *Young Voices* film, "If you adults won't do something about global climate change, then we kids are going to take the reins." Kids absolutely can take effective action against climate change, and they are doing it now all over the world. Moreover, their empowered responses are helping these youth feel *less* defeated by the climate crisis and *better* about themselves.

The *Young Voices for the Planet* films are changing the face of climate change education by replacing fear with action. The dynamic youth portrayed in the films exhibit many qualities that foster success. For example, these youth know how to work collaboratively with peers, teachers, school administrators, government and businesses officials, and others. They show that it's possible to address climate change by identifying win-win solutions for all stakeholders.

The *Young Voices* educational approach rests on solid research and observation. For a decade, scientists and educators assumed that if people understood the seriousness of the climate crisis, they would act. But, in fact, the more scientific information people heard, the stronger was their denial. Various studies have shed light on why people avoid accepting the facts about climate change: psychologically, they just cannot handle the disturbing truth. Instead of motivating them to learn more and act, learning about frightening natural hazards generally motivates people to *avoid* learning more science! In 2012, a study in the *Journal of Personality and Social Psychology* named this response to frightening facts "motivated avoidance."[1]

A study by Professor Anthony Leiserowitz, director of the Yale Project on Climate Change Communication, revealed similar findings. Leiserowitz found that climate-related images invoking fear produced a strong negative affect and actually impeded people from accepting climate change science.[2] These studies and others make it clear that factual information alone cannot be the basis of climate change education.

But ignoring the problem is no way to calm students' fears either. Research shows that children who are not allowed to discuss and process fears are actually more fearful than children who have the opportunity to express their thoughts and fears.

So we must rethink how to teach climate change. The approach used in the *Young Voices for the Planet* films and in this teaching guide is gaining currency among educators who had, in the past, unwittingly scared students into "motivated avoidance." Our approach encompasses the key strategies described below.

ELEMENTS OF *YOUNG VOICES* CLIMATE CHANGE EDUCATION

Storytelling

Everyone is captivated by a good story, and each *Young Voices for the Planet* film tells an inspiring one. Even better, these stories are true! Each film profiles real-life characters and presents moving tales of challenge and success. The films are nonfictional but are told in an entertaining narrative style. After all, they are produced by Lynne Cherry, acclaimed children's book author and storyteller. (See the note from Lynne about the origin of the *Young Voices for the Planet* films on page 10.)

Positive Role-Modeling

The students profiled in the films live in different places, have strikingly different personalities and circumstances, and offer diverse ideas about how to preserve Earth's life-sustaining climate. Nevertheless, each exhibits qualities universally admired, such as compassion, responsibility, caring, creativity, and the ability to collaborate. Regardless of how students identify themselves culturally—whether they are into sports, student government, video games, art, hanging out at the mall, or none of the above—they are sure to find role models they admire and can relate to in the *Young Voices* films.

Climate Change Portrayed as Real, Present, and Relevant

As we all know, students complain about curriculum that makes them wonder, "Why do I need to know this?" Irrelevant curriculum is perceived as boring and meaningless. But the truth is that climate change science is all too relevant. Presented in the right way, it's an extremely compelling topic because the stakes are high and time is running short. It is perhaps the most meaningful, relevant, and important topic that you will teach in your lifetime. In our approach to teaching climate change, we do not suggest that you waffle or downplay the urgency of the issue so as to avoid alarming your students. Rather, we hope you will invite your students into the awareness that the climate needs our protection—now!

Solutions, Not Scary Scenarios

There is clear consensus among scientists that climate change threatens human civilization. Many effects of our warming climate have been forecast, and this program invites students to learn about them. In particular, we encourage students to investigate climate predictions relating to the places where they live. This being said, it's imperative that you avoid dwelling on possible negative outcomes. Rather, we give you tools to support students in their creativity, problem solving, and resolve to do something. Part I of this teaching guide gives you an array of activity ideas to keep the focus on student empowerment and growth, and Part II supports your efforts to build a custom project.

Science Integrated With Social Studies, Literature, Math, the Arts, and More

As we have noted, climate change education needs to involve the whole student—hand, heart, and mind—rather than just the intellect. Thus the *Young Voices* program is thoroughly subject integrated.

Practical Skill Building and How-to Tips

Changing the world takes practical skills and savvy as well as positive intentions. So Part I of this teaching guide is replete with activities that build science process skills such as observing, estimating, predicting, and inferring. Skills for civic engagement are needed too, so students will learn how to write letters to business and government officials, how to contact news and other media outlets, how to employ social networking, how to convene public meetings, how to analyze issues and the claims of experts in the media for accuracy, and so on.

Correlation to Standards

The Next Generation Science Standards (NGSS) are clear about the importance of climate science in school curriculum. Also, the Common Core contains mathematics and literacy standards that support interdisciplinary curricula such as climate change science. Thus there are many ways in which the *Young Voices for the Planet* program satisfies Common Core as well as NGSS. A few standards that *Young Voices* supports are listed here in the box headed "Standards." A more complete list is included in Appendix II.

STANDARDS

Sample NGSS: Disciplinary Core Ideas

ESS3.C: Human Impacts on Earth Systems

- Human activities in agriculture, industry, and everyday life have had major effects on the land, vegetation, streams, ocean, air, and even outer space. But individuals and communities are doing things to help protect Earth's resources and environments. (5-ESS3-1)

- Human activities have significantly altered the biosphere, sometimes damaging or destroying natural habitats and causing the extinction of other species. But changes to Earth's environments can have different impacts (negative and positive) for different living things. (MS-ESS3-3)

- Typically as human populations and per-capita consumption of natural resources increase, so do the negative impacts on Earth unless the activities and technologies involved are engineered otherwise. (MS-ESS3-3), (MS-ESS3-4)

ESS3.D: Global Climate Change

- Human activities, such as the release of greenhouse gases from burning fossil fuels, are major factors in the current rise in Earth's mean surface temperature (global warming). Reducing the level of climate change and reducing human vulnerability to whatever climate changes do occur depend on the understanding of climate science, engineering capabilities, and other kinds of knowledge, such as understanding of human behavior and on applying that knowledge wisely in decisions and activities. (MS-ESS3-5)

Sample Common Core English Language Arts Standards: Science and Technical Subjects

Integration of Knowledge and Ideas

CCSS.ELA-Literacy.RST.6-8.7

- Integrate quantitative or technical information expressed in words in a text with a version of that information expressed visually (e.g., in a flowchart, diagram, model, graph, or table).

CCSS.ELA-Literacy.RST.6-8.8

- Distinguish among facts, reasoned judgment based on research findings, and speculation in a text.

CCSS.ELA-Literacy.RST.6-8.9

- Compare and contrast the information gained from experiments, simulations, video, or multimedia sources with that gained from reading a text on the same topic.

Humor and Fun

Humor can help to dispel the anxiety of hearing heavy messages about climate change and grab the attention of a youthful audience, enabling students to *hear* the message. For example, when the kids in the *Team Marine* film dress up as plastic-bag and bottle-cap monsters and galumph down the street in slow motion, the audience erupts in rollicking laughter. Such comic relief provides a welcome counterpoint to outright disgusting images of plastic marine debris killing sea turtles and ocean birds. Likewise, many activities in this teaching guide involve art and expression, and team-building exercises such as cooperative games. In serious times, it's sometimes important to lighten up!

Collaboration and Community

Truly, protecting Earth's climate will require contributions from everyone—not just a certain social group. Everyone has a different piece of the puzzle and everyone is important. The notion of "leaders" and "followers" doesn't make much sense when all kinds of projects on every scale are needed and when big projects need people to carry out plans as much as they need people to formulate them. The spirit of climate change activism—and this program—is cooperative!

Self-Efficacy

The *Young Voices for the Planet* program nurtures young people's *self-efficacy,* their faith in their own ability to create change. Achieving self-efficacy is valuable lifetime learning. Self-efficacy is a big part of how people think of themselves and an important component of mental health. Building self-efficacy will help students for the rest of their lives!

A key to teaching youth about climate change is to encourage them to think critically and to take action on what they've learned. As they observe that they do have power to take meaningful action, their sense of self-efficacy grows. Further, building self-efficacy is an iterative process. That is, the more empowered a student feels, the more she can do—and the more she accomplishes, the higher her sense of self-efficacy rises, and the more she can do next time. This is a virtuous cycle.

Albert Bandura of Stanford University (Department of Psychology) is credited with developing self-efficacy theory. He has documented how "efficacy beliefs" affect the way individuals perceive their ability to create personal and social change. In his book *Self-Efficacy: The Exercise of*

Control, Bandura states: "Efficacy beliefs shape the outcomes people expect their efforts to produce. . . . People of low self-efficacy are easily convinced of the futility of effort in the face of impediments. Those of high self-efficacy view impediments as surmountable through perseverance."[3]

Bandura's research also shows that young people's beliefs regarding their ability to change things affect their emotional lives and how much stress, anxiety, and depression they experience in threatening or disheartening situations. Those who believe they can manage problems and adversity view life as less threatening and take action to change things. So developing self-efficacy in young people helps in their personal growth and in their role as global citizens.

As previously discussed, studies show that scaring students with frightening information about climate change makes them less likely to want to learn more and act. Students become overwhelmed, a state that is bad for them and bad for a warming world. But self-efficacy theory shows us a way out. If students believe they can make a difference, they will be motivated to learn more and act. Building self-efficacy and learning about climate change must go hand in hand, or else despair or denial will likely result.

Bandura's book describes three ways to build self-efficacy, and the *Young Voices for the Planet* educational program employs them all. They are as follows:

1. Building mastery. This is the most effective way to strengthen self-efficacy. Let students act and support them so that they can view their actions as successful. For example, if your students learn how trees remove CO_2 from the atmosphere and then plant trees, they will have taken a successful first step toward reducing climate change and this will help them build mastery.

2. Social modeling. If people can relate to others they see taking actions, they are likely to believe that they can, too. The diversity of students profiled in the *Young Voices for the Planet* films allows students to see their peers—students like themselves—making a difference, which can lead them to think that they can, too. As Olivia Bouler states in *Olivia's Birds and the Oil Spill,* "If they can do that, then so can I." In *Plant for the Planet,* Felix, an eleven-year-old German boy, starts a website that goes viral and leads to worldwide youth planting billions of trees. Often a child will feel that he or she is as irrelevant as one small raindrop, but many raindrops make a stream and then a river. Felix's campaign allows youth to see themselves as a river of young people creating an ocean of change. Thus watching the *Young Voices* films jump-starts students' self-efficacy, boosting their confidence and desire to act.

3. Social persuasion. If your students are persuaded that success is possible, if they say, "I think I can," they work harder than if the voices in their heads say, "I can't do it." The youth activists in the *Young Voices for the Planet* films model self-efficacy and faith in others' capabilities too, all of which makes success more likely.

In summary, based on research and experience, we believe that climate change education works best when it builds self-efficacy at the same time it builds knowledge. Without the opportunity to act and the confidence to do so, students tend to default into despair or denial when faced with the challenges associated with climate change. We ask: How can a teacher build self-efficacy in her students? And we answer that question with Bandura's finding that "mastery" builds self-efficacy most powerfully. But social persuasion and social modeling can work too, and they certainly get students headed in the right direction. *Young Voices* pedagogy uses all three roads to self-efficacy. And that is why it works!

Finally, a couple of quotes on the importance of self-efficacy:

> The most common way people give up their power is by thinking they don't have any.
>
> —Alice Walker

> The world will not be destroyed by those who do evil but by those who watch them without doing anything.
>
> —Albert Einstein

The *Young Voices for the Planet* climate change program is a comprehensive platform with multiple learning resources. The films and this teaching guide are parts of a larger strategy that we have developed as part of a multimedia platform including K–12 curricula, the book *How We Know What We Know About Our Changing Climate,* a website with downloadable resources, television programming, catalog distribution to schools and libraries, and many other components.

How did this multifaceted project get started? More than a decade ago, Gary Braasch, renowned environmental photojournalist, began documenting weather extremes and polar melting as well as interviewing climate scientists worldwide. His book *Earth Under Fire: How Global Warming Is Changing the World* was one of the first books that vividly made the case that humankind needs to act now to counter global warming.[4] Braasch's book spawned the award-winning children's book *How We Know What We Know About Our Changing Climate,* coauthored by

Braasch and Lynne Cherry.[5] Cherry, the producer of the *Young Voices* films and coauthor of this teaching guide, is an environmental writer/ illustrator and author of the *The Great Kapok Tree, A River Ran Wild,* and thirty other popular children's books. The book that Cherry and Braasch wrote together on climate won fifteen major awards, including Best Science Book for Middle Schoolers from the American Association for the Advancement of Science.

As successful as the Cherry-Braasch book was, Cherry wanted to do more to help youth grapple with the issue of Earth's warming climate in a positive, inspiring format. Hence the *Young Voices for the Planet* films were born, as described here in the "Note From Lynne Cherry." Now this teaching guide, coauthored by Cherry and veteran science educators Juliana Texley and Suzanne Lyons, expands the power of the *Young Voices for the Planet* films with concrete teaching strategies, activities, and how-to information. Enjoy!

Source: Lynne Cherry in Australian rainforest. Photo by Gary Braasch from *How We Know What We Know About Our Changing Climate.*

MISSION STATEMENT

The mission of the *Young Voices for the Planet* climate change program is to give young people a means to speak out, create solutions, and lead the change to a more sustainable future.

A NOTE FROM LYNNE CHERRY

When Gary Braasch and I wrote our book *How We Know What We Know About Our Changing Climate: Scientists and Kids Explore Global Warming,* we believed that we were writing a hopeful book. We included stores of young people doing research similar to that of the scientists on the Intergovernmental Panel on Climate Change. And we included success stories of young people reducing CO_2 emissions. But, after hearing from educators, we realized that our positive empowering messages needed to be even stronger. Teachers needed concrete models for replication.

To this end, we produced a series of films, *Young Voices for the Planet,* that introduce climate science through success stories of young people reducing the carbon footprints of their homes, schools, and communities. These stories of empowered youth also demonstrate that, as thirteen-year-old Alec Loorz says, "Kids have power." The films embrace diversity; the young people in these films, from across the ethnic, geographic, and socioeconomic spectrum, have an earnestness and a sincerity that touches our hearts. As Anya Suslova from Siberia stated emphatically, but with a smile, "You can make a difference, so do something!"

PART

It's Happening Now All Over the World

Earth's average temperature has risen about 1.3°F over the past century—a sudden increase that's extremely rare over Earth's 4.6-billion-year history. Why the temperature increase? The cause is basically the greenhouse effect. In the greenhouse effect, carbon dioxide and other greenhouse gases trap heat in Earth's lower atmosphere, and this warms the planet. Since the 1850s, the concentration of atmospheric greenhouse gases has risen sharply, in step with increasing consumption of fossil fuels. In addition to fossil fuel use, deforestation is a major cause of increased atmospheric CO_2, enhanced greenhouse effect, and a warmer Earth. Trees that would remove CO_2 from the atmosphere are cut down and are therefore no longer around to help absorb this greenhouse gas.

The effects of Earth's one-degree temperature rise are already with us. Drought, flooding, wildfires, hurricanes, sea-level rise, changes in currents, melting permafrost, and the extinction of some species as well as the northward and upward migration of others are just some of the effects.

Even more ominous is the fact that the warming is accelerating. The Intergovernmental Panel on Climate Change, or IPCC, is probably the world's leading authority on climate change. It is made up of more than 1,300 scientists from around the world who volunteer to review the credible scientific research on climate. The IPCC predicts that Earth's average temperature will increase between 2.5°F (1.4°C) and 10°F (5.6°C) over the next century, depending on human activities. If a one-degree rise has caused the effects we are observing now, you can imagine that a temperature rise of several degrees more could be catastrophic indeed! The time to start reducing CO_2 emissions and preserving the world's forests to stabilize climate is now.

Earth's lower atmosphere contains many substances, including *greenhouse gases* (such as carbon dioxide, methane, and water vapor). Greenhouse gases are important to temperature because they allow light energy from the sun to pass through them. Visible light, or "shortwave electromagnetic radiation," thus passes through the atmosphere and is absorbed once it reaches Earth's surface. Some of this incoming energy is retained by the ground and warms it. However, much of the incoming shortwave radiation is not absorbed by the ground. Instead, it is reemitted as longer-wavelength infrared radiation by Earth's surface. But unlike shortwave radiation—that is, visible light—the longer-wavelength infrared radiation cannot easily escape Earth's atmosphere since greenhouse gas molecules absorb it. So, due to greenhouse gases, infrared radiation is retained in the lower atmosphere, and this increases Earth's temperature.

The greenhouse effect is actually a natural and necessary phenomenon. Without it, the atmosphere would be a frigid −18°C. The present concern is about the *anthropogenic greenhouse effect. Anthropogenic* means "human caused." The global average temperature rise observed over the past century correlates with increased levels of greenhouse gases in the atmosphere, which in turn result from certain human activities, especially the increased consumption of fossil fuels. Thus the enhanced greenhouse effect today, which has led to higher temperatures, is known to be anthropogenic rather than naturally caused.

A good place for youth to begin is with the film *Kids vs Global Warming* and the following activity. It integrates a bit of mathematics as an "appetizer." It shows students that small actions can add up to big gains for the planet.

INTRO ACTIVITY: TRAINS, PLANES, AND AUTOMOBILES

Show your students the trailer for the film *Kids vs Global Warming*. Point out that producer Lynne Cherry introduces an important theme—transportation. We see her on an Amtrak train riding from Washington, D.C., to Los Angeles, California. She has decided to skip driving and avoid flying. Why?

Pose the following problem: *Estimate how much carbon dioxide is not released into the atmosphere as a result of Lynne's choice to take the train.* Give students the following facts:

- The distance from Washington, D.C., to Los Angeles, California, is about 2,700 miles.

- A passenger plane gets about 23 passenger miles per gallon if it is full. The average car gets about 21 miles per gallon on the open highway. A passenger train gets about 45 passenger miles per gallon.

- Combusting a gallon of gasoline releases about 20 pounds (9 kg) of carbon dioxide into the atmosphere.

Answer

If Lynne had driven, she would have used 129 gallons of gas for the trip; if she had flown she would have used about 117 gallons; by taking the train she used 60 gallons. Therefore, by taking the train, Lynne saved the atmosphere 1,140 pounds of CO_2 versus a plane and 1,380 pounds of CO_2 versus a car. (See Appendix II for full calculations.)

Discussion

Brainstorm with students all of the factors that enter into estimating the true fossil fuel consumption in miles per gallon for various modes of transportation. For example, airplane travel requires not just the plane but the energy needed to run the airport. Driving a car 2,700 miles often means meals in restaurants and nights spent in hotels. So the use of planes and cars actually costs more energy than stated here. On the other hand, trains sometimes include both passenger cars and freight cars, so their efficiency can be greater than the "bare numbers" indicate. Trains are the most energy-efficient way to move products and passengers across the country. Even when students understand that their calculations are by necessity just estimates, the calculations here lead to the correct conclusions about the efficiency of trains, planes, and single-passenger cars.

Common Core: Estimation

CCSS.Math.Content.3

- Solve problems involving measurement and estimation.

CCSS.Math.Content.4.NBT.A.3

- Use place value understanding to round multi-digit whole numbers to any place: Estimate differences.

CCSS.Math.Content.7

- Solve real-life and mathematical problems using numerical and algebraic expressions and equations: Estimate sums, differences, and products using decimals.

NGSS: Practices of Science

1. Asking questions (for science) and defining problems (for engineering)
2. Developing and using models
3. Planning and carrying out investigations
4. Analyzing and interpreting data
5. Using mathematics and computational thinking
6. Constructing explanations (for science) and designing solutions (for engineering)
7. Engaging in argument from evidence
8. Obtaining, evaluating, and communicating information

Notes

Alec Loorz
Kids vs Global Warming

Activities in This Chapter:

Activity 1.1. STEAM It Up! Communicate Through the Arts

Activity 1.2. Researching Climate Change—Many Methods, Many Mentors

Activity 1.3. Rising Sea Levels, Sinking Hopes

It's hard to predict what will start a fire in youth. For twelve-year-old Alec Loorz, it was Al Gore's documentary movie *An Inconvenient Truth*. The specter of global climate change wouldn't fade away for him.

Alec's mother was his first mentor. She understood. She didn't suggest that his ideas were unrealistic or too big for one person to tackle. She helped him arrange a meeting with paleoclimatologist Richard Norris of the Scripps Institute in San Diego, California. At Scripps, Alec saw evidence of Earth's climate in ancient ice cores and got answers to some of his questions. He also met climate researcher Lisa Shaffer.

Alec's mentors respected his energy and his enthusiasm. Feeling the weight of the global situation and a sense that he could make a difference, Alec felt compelled to tell other kids about the problems he saw. Eventually he was invited by Al Gore to be formally trained with the Climate Project in October 2008. He has given more than 150 presentations on global warming—reaching almost 75,000 in his audiences. In the film *Kids vs Global Warming,* we see young Alec creating presentations specifically for youth. As this book goes to print, Alec is eighteen and in college in Canada. He has been a keynote speaker at conferences such as Bioneers and TED and at the United Nations. And he has won many awards for his work trying to move people to speak out for taking action on climate change. In fact, Alec and other youth brought a lawsuit against every U.S. state government for failing to regulate carbon emissions and protect their future. In his spare time, he creates presentations

Alec raised public awareness with sea-level awareness posts (SLAPs) to show where the water level would be with different degrees of warming. Young people in New York drew a blue line along city streets to show what would be submerged by the elevated water. What kinds of signposts or symbols can you create in order to engage your community? If you live by the ocean, you might create signs that depict sea-level rise. If you live by an inland lake, the water level will go down! (That's because warmer temperatures make less ice cover; with less ice cover, lake water evaporates faster in the winter, emptying the lake.)

If your community isn't near a conspicuous body of water, students can create visual symbols representing many other climate change effects. Will the balance among the common types of trees—the climax community—change? Will there be more erosion or fires? More carbon dioxide means more "C_4" plants like Kudzu and poison ivy and more heat-adapted animals like mosquitoes!

Once your students have created visual images of the near future, hold a gathering such as a "poetry slam," gallery walk, or video festival.

Are students' signs "ready for prime time"? If so, post them where they will have an impact in the community. Alec erected his SLAPs along the ocean promenade. Ask business owners to post the signs in windows and on community bulletin boards.

• • •

specifically for youth, full of videos, animation, and easy-to-understand science. His message is deeply rooted in hope, encouraging kids to speak up and let their voices be heard on this issue.

Mentors were crucial for Alec Loorz. But who is a mentor? While we most often think of scientists as mentors for science students, in your own community a mentor might be anyone who will listen! A mentor can be anyone—the teacher, the media specialist, the senior volunteer. The most important requirement for the role is a willingness to take the enthusiasm and the curiosity of young climate investigators seriously.

What *isn't* required? A white lab coat, a single scientific method, or a "smarter than thou" attitude. Mentors may need to inject some realistic caution and courtesy when the enthusiasm of one young voice or many spills over, but they should never be discouraging: "You may not be able to do all that right away, but what parts of your ideas are realistic first steps?" Many great efforts have begun with brainstorming and diagrams "on the back of an envelope."

Mentors are especially helpful for marginalized or disadvantaged students. It's important for everyone to recognize that climate advocates are diverse and creative. While climate change science can get very complex, its main ideas are quite simple. That's what Activity 1.2 will help students see. No matter what their skills and science acumen, all students have something to contribute to protecting the climate.

The Web quest in Activity 1.2 begins with five scientists who have worked with young people who have high aspirations. You might want to add others who you think could be relevant role models for your particular students. Scientists do make great mentors—but be sure to interpret the term *scientist* liberally. Science takes many forms, and mentors have many opportunities to guide youth through various applications of science.

Like Alec Loorz, your own students are looking for mentors. Once they've identified resources and people who might be able to help them on their journeys, encourage them to be bold. There are many, many researchers who—like Richard Norris—are happy to help youth get started.

In Activity 1.2, students imagine what it would be like if some of the "big-name" climate researchers were their mentors.

Sea-level rise is one of the effects of climate change that is already here and growing worse. It's a topic of obvious concern to people living along the world's coastlines, such as Alec Loorz. Sea level rises when the temperature of the ocean increases because seawater expands as it warms. Also, melting glaciers add water to the sea.

Each of the scientists listed below is involved in some aspect of climate change research. In this activity, students research the scientists. They find out one problem that each scientist researched or is researching, and they find out one method that the scientist has used. Students then imagine they could meet this scientist and ask him or her a question of interest.

Some of these scientists are profiled in the book *How We Know What We Know About Our Changing Climate: Scientists and Kids Explore Global Warming.* Students can use the Internet to research the scientists as well.

The student sheet corresponding to this activity appears in Appendix I. Copy it and distribute one sheet to each student.

TABLE 1.2.1 Climate Scientists and Their Research

SCIENTIST	PROBLEM	SCIENCE PRACTICES	QUESTION YOU WOULD ASK
Richard Norris			
Terry Root			
Steve Schneider			
Lisa Shaffer			
James Hansen			

Alec Loorz
Kids vs. Global Warming

In this exercise, students analyze sea-level rise using topographic maps. Provide each student with a copy of Student Sheet 1.3. Also provide each student with six colored pencils, each of a different color.

In the first part of the activity, students examine the following topographical map of Manhattan Island, New York. They color-code the regions that would be flooded if sea level rose in 1-meter increments up to 6 meters. Explain that a 6-meter rise in sea level is a worst-case scenario and is not predicted to occur during this century. According to the Intergovernmental Panel on Climate Change, a 6-meter rise would occur if the entire Greenland ice sheet were to melt. The IPCC predicts that the most likely sea-level rise by 2100 is between 80 centimeters and 1 meter. Longer term, however, sea level will continue to rise even after CO_2 emissions have been reduced or eliminated.

Students will see that a 1-meter sea-level rise would flood a large land area. A 2- to 3-meter rise would also flood large areas. After that, 1-meter increments of sea-level rise would flood smaller geographic areas.

You may need to discuss topographic maps with your students in advance of this activity. If so, share the following information: A topographic map is a map that shows the elevation of Earth's surface features. Elevation is the height of something above sea level. The elevation of sea level is 0. Topographic maps, or "topos," show elevation with contour lines.

FIGURE 1.3.1

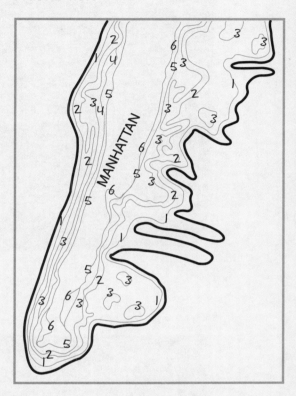

Contour lines are lines that connect places that are at the same elevation.

Call students' attention to the topographic map of Manhattan on the student sheet. Have them examine its contour lines. Tell them that the contour lines on the map reflect the shape of the land because they connect points of equal elevation.

After examining New York, students examine a map indicating sea-level rise in Florida. They identify the cities that are flooded at various increments of sea-level rise.

• • •

STANDARDS

Notes

2 Girl Scouts

Lighting the Community

Activity in This Chapter:

Activity 2.1. Check It Out

For Clarissa Klein and Hannah Poplack, "Be prepared" isn't just a motto. It's a guide to a brighter future. Their Girl Scout troop was instrumental in distributing more than five thousand compact fluorescent lightbulbs (CFLs) in their community. CFLs represent engineering innovation with the potential to have a significant positive impact on our "carbon footprint" and on Earth's atmosphere. These bulbs can replace the traditional incandescent lightbulbs that we've used—and overused—for more than a century. They typically have a life of 6,000 to 15,000 hours, compared to 750–1,000 hours for the typical old-fashioned bulb, and they use just one-third to one-seventh the energy. While CFLs contain minute amounts of mercury and so must be carefully recycled, the mercury produced by power plants that fuel those old-fashioned lightbulbs is hundreds of times greater. (Note that there is now a newer energy-efficient light source based on LED technology. Bulbs that incorporate LEDs, or light-emitting diodes, use even less energy than CFLs, and they contain no mercury! They are currently relatively expensive—but look for improvements to LED bulbs coming soon.)

The bulbs distributed by the Girl Scouts were provided by the Sierra Club, and the Scouts' initiative brought the bulbs into use. With smiles and positive messages the Scouts were able to convince families in their community to try something new. Families who started using the new bulbs were likely to continue, so the impact of the Scouts' efforts is likely to be greater and more long-lasting than anyone can calculate.

How much did the troop accomplish in energy savings? You can use a convenient online calculator to estimate that. But it isn't just a matter of numbers. By helping their community accept one practical engineering solution, they also opened up the possibility of more team partnerships to engineer a better future. People are sometimes hesitant to change even if it's good for them. By giving out the new bulbs for free, these Girl Scouts made change easier for thousands of people who could then experience a win-win example—saving money while also saving the world.

National Geographic provides a convenient online calculator that can determine how much energy is saved with CFLs and LEDs as opposed to old-fashioned incandescent lightbulbs. It also provides another calculator that can help people determine—and reduce—their carbon footprints.

Provide students with Internet access. Send them to the lightbulb energy calculator at this address:

http://environment.nationalgeographic.com/environment/energy/great-energy-challenge/light-bulb-savings-calculator

Pose the following questions to your students:

Suppose there are 50 lightbulbs in your house. Also suppose that 18 of them are incandescent bulbs, 16 of them are CFLs, and 16 of them are LED bulbs.

1. How much money are you saving each year on energy due to your choice of bulbs?

2. If every household in the United States used the same bulbs as you, what would be the national savings in energy costs?

3. Fill in the blank: This energy savings would be like shutting _____ coal power plants down.

• • •

Sample NGSS Disciplinary Core Idea

ETS1.B: Developing Possible Solutions

- A solution needs to be tested, and then modified on the basis of the test results, in order to improve it. (MS-ETS1-4)

- There are systematic processes for evaluating solutions with respect to how well they meet the criteria and constraints of a problem. (MS-ETS1-2), (MS-ETS1-3)

- Sometimes parts of different solutions can be combined.

3 Team Marine and a Time Machine

Activities in This Chapter:

It's hard to find a place on the planet where you can't find them—from a mountain in Ethiopia to doldrums in the center of the Pacific Ocean. Plastic bags! But there are a lot fewer in Santa Monica, California, due to the actions of Team Marine. This group's activism caused an entire community to ban plastic grocery bags. That action served as a model for many other communities in California and across the globe.

How did it begin? With observation. First the students studied plastic bags and the plastic bits on the beach. Marine animals are constantly dying from ingestion of plastic or from being trapped in it. Endangered sea turtles mistake floating bags for jellyfish, their main source of food. Seabirds suffocate when their necks become stuck in the plastic rings from six-packs of soda. Plastic lasts almost forever! Americans use 2.5 million plastic bottles every hour! Recycling one plastic bottle can save enough energy to power a 60-watt lightbulb for six hours. By one estimate, you might find a single bottle (in a decomposer-rich landfill) still intact for seven hundred years.

The members of Team Marine continued their fight to eliminate plastic bags in their community with humor and persistence. They prepared their case, made their presentations, and won their votes. Their impact: five plastic bags = 2.2 pounds (1 kg) of carbon dioxide in the atmosphere. By using one less bag per day, each person could prevent 161 pounds (73 kg) of carbon dioxide from going into the atmosphere. The entire U.S. population (almost 310 million, according to the 2010 census) would thus prevent about 23 billion kg of carbon dioxide from being emitted each year. Further, according to the U.S. Environmental Protection Agency, the equivalent of nine barrels of oil is saved when we recycle 1 ton (907 kg) of plastic bags. A plastic bag weighs about 6 g., so if every person in the United States used one less plastic bag per day on average, a total of 6.2 million barrels of oil would be saved. Banning plastic bags from an entire community saves wildlife, oil, and the climate in a big way!

Young Voices for the Planet and Urban EcoLab Curriculum have teamed up to bring you a large variety of hands-on activities. Check out http://www.youngvoicesonclimatechange.com and browse by film to find activities for your class. The following activity is especially recommended.

Students can begin to investigate the first step in the plastic recycling process—separating different types of plastic by density—if your school has the appropriate laboratory settings to do Activity 3.3 safely. You will need to provide students with shreds of common plastics. (If you elect to let students shred the plastic, they will need gloves and impact eye protection.) You will also need to provide students with the solutions listed

FIGURE 3.1.1

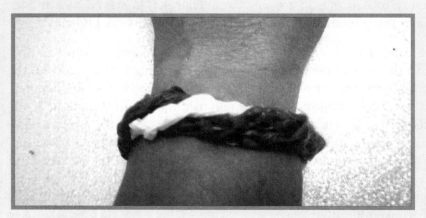

The best way to counter the effect of plastic bags is not to use them at all. But those that are around anyway can be repurposed. They can be made into a crafty "reminder bracelet" like the one shown here—to remind us to reuse and recycle!

Cut three colors of bags into long strips approximately 1.5 cm wide. Knit the strips into thick chains, then braid the three chains into a bracelet. *Extra:* Work in wooden beads that say "Recycle." Don't use plastic beads, because if such beads end up in the ocean they are harmful to sea life! Buying anything plastic is problematic, not only because of the petrochemicals used to make it but also because of the length of time that plastic remains in the environment. What happens to those plastic items you put into the recycling bin? Think you are recycling? Think again. Almost half of the plastic currently put into recycling bins doesn't get recycled at all because we don't yet have the right technology to make it practical. So the best choice is always to avoid creating a market for plastic in the first place.

● ● ●

The Urban EcoLab Curriculum contains online lessons to support this content area. Go to the Web address below to browse. We highly recommend Module 4, Lesson 2, which covers the concepts of waste and garbage. You can choose from three different activities in Module 4, Lesson 2, or do them all. The first activity enables students to distinguish between biodegradable and nonbiodegradable garbage. The second activity concerns methods of garbage disposal. The third activity is a debate that connects waste disposal to social justice.

Go to http://urbanecolabcurriculum.com/ modules/module-4/module-4-lesson-2- where-does-our-garbage-go.

in Table 3.3.1. You will most likely want to make up the solutions yourself. For work with all chemicals, eye protection for chemical splash is required. (A lengthier version of this activity and many other recycling activities can be found on the website of the Institute of Scrap Recycling Industries, at http://www.ISRI.org.)

The next activity supporting the film *Team Marine and a Time Machine* lets students see that trash—especially plastic—takes a very long time to decompose. It's an observational activity that ideally runs over several months. When it comes to garbage, there is no such thing as throwing it "away."

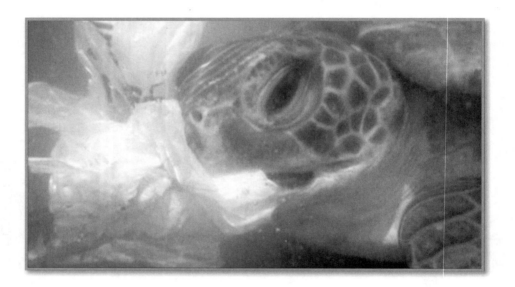

WHAT HAPPENS TO WHAT'S IN THE RECYCLING BIN?

Hand out one copy of Student Sheet 3.3 to each student.

Explain to students that at least seven kinds of plastics are common in the home. Much plastic can be recycled, although with current technology, the process is not a simple one. Sometimes the plastic we put into recycling bins isn't recycled after all because the process is not cost-effective. So the best path always is to not use plastic at all. But if you do, understanding the process is important. In order to begin recycling, processors must separate the seven different kinds of plastic. They normally do this by shredding the plastic and then separating the shreds by density.

In this activity, students drop shreds of various plastics into five solutions. They observe which shreds sink or float in which solutions. They can thereby determine the density range of each "mystery shred" and compare it to the densities of known plastics to identify each shred.

Be sure to remind (or explain to) your students how density relates to flotation: If a material floats, its density is less than the density of the surrounding fluid. If it sinks, the material is denser than the surrounding fluid.

Use Table 3.3.1 to make up solutions for your students. The amounts stated are for one student team, so scale up as needed to provide for your entire class.

TABLE 3.3.1 Solutions for Testing the Density of Plastics

SOLUTION	AMOUNT ALCOHOL	AMOUNT WATER	AMOUNT SUGAR	MASS	DENSITY
1	100 mL	40 mL			.91 g/mL
2	80 mL	40 mL			.93 g/mL
3		150 mL			1.0 g/mL
4	150 mL				0.78 g/mL
5		150 mL	75 g		1.14 g/mL

The densities of common plastics are as follows:

PETE (polyethylene terephthalate)	1.38 g/mL	PS (polystyrene)	1.06 g/mL
HDPE (high-density polyethylene)	0.95 g/mL	Lexan (polycarbonate)	1.2 g/mL
LDPE (low-density polyethylene)	0.94 g/mL	PVC (polyvinyl chloride)	1.16–1.38 g/mL
PP (polypropylene)	0.91 g/mL		

Activity 3.4

THE TRASH TIME MACHINE

Hand out a copy of Student Sheet 3.4 to each student. Supply trowels or shovels so students can dig a hole in the soil outside the classroom. Supply typical garbage items that students can put into the pit they have dug. For example, you might use

- A plastic water bottle
- A plastic grocery bag
- A paper cup or plate
- A fruit or vegetable
- A preserved food snack (such as Twinkies)
- Cotton cloth (such as a rag or T-shirt)
- A piece of wood

Students bury the trash items with the intention of checking on them later in the school year.

When the garbage pit has been dug, have students answer these questions:

1. How long will it take for each item to decompose? Check your predictions at the end of the year.

2. How is the observation pit you built like a landfill? How is it different?

Also ask students to solve the following problem, which is stated on the student sheet too.

Given that there are *308,745,538* people living in the United States (2010 census), how much trash do the American people "throw away"? Calculate:

1. If each person used one plastic water bottle a day, how many bottles would be used in the United States in a year?

2. Find the mass of a single empty plastic water bottle. How many tons of plastic would one-a-day use by every person in the United States produce in a year?

3. Use the Internet to determine how long a plastic water bottle lasts.

4. If you could influence 30 people to give up using plastic water bottles for a year, how much less plastic would your great-grandchildren have to clean up?

● ● ●

Sample NGSS Disciplinary Core Idea

MS-ESS3-4: Earth and Human Activity

- Construct an argument supported by evidence for how increases in human population and per-capita consumption of natural resources impact Earth's systems.

4

Anya
Citizen Science in Siberia

Activities in This Chapter:

What is science? Why is it important to me? It's not enough to just tell a student the answers. When students find out the answers for themselves, nothing can stop them from putting science to good use.

Anya is a thirteen-year-old indigenous girl from the Russian village of Zhigansk. She sees her world melting away due to warming caused by the developed world's CO_2 emissions. She joins Arctic scientist Max Holmes's Long Term Ecological Research (LTER) team, which is studying the effects of melting ice on the Lena River. (See the LTER Network's site at http://www.lternet.edu and Holmes's Polar Field Services site at http://www.polarfield.com/blog/tag/nsf-arctic-research-program.) Through LTER, Anya learns about global warming. Anya then teaches her schoolmates and traditional community elders about the effects of climate change. All through the Arctic winter she drills holes through the ice in order to collect water samples for Max Holmes and his research team.

Like citizens all over the world, Anya is discovering clues about climate change in her own area of the planet. In doing her work, Anya discovers the following:

- The scientific process
- How scientists formulate answerable questions
- How scientists take samples and measurements
- What scientists can learn from samples and measurements

Many people believe that using the term *global warming* contributes to misunderstandings and makes it more difficult for people to see the signs of climate change in their own areas. Climate change involves much more than just an increase in average global temperature. While the average temperature all over the planet is rising, local effects can vary. For example, sea-level rise directly affects people living in island or coastal communities. People in the vicinity of the Great Lakes observe falling lake levels due to lack of winter ice cover and increased evaporation. States in the eastern region of the United States flood, and western states burn. The frequency of different kinds of extreme weather events—from hurricanes to heat waves—is different in different places. Currently, Anya is attending college in India where she is studying ecology and political science. It takes thousands of citizen scientists like Anya working in different places to "ground truth" the effects of too much carbon dioxide in our atmosphere.

In Activity 4.3, students identify areas of nutrient-enriched effluent on a world map. Then they form hypotheses regarding why productivity changes in various areas of the ocean.

For centuries, communities have joined to make quilts. The process is easy, and it lends itself to sharing among diverse communities too.

First share with your students an award-winning book about habitats: *Nature's Habitat Quilt,* by Mary Miché (2012).

Ask the students to create the blocks of their own "habitat quilt" for your local area. Provide each student with a square of pre-shrunk and dye-ready cotton. Ask each to choose one organism in the area to illustrate for the quilt. Don't forget the plants and decomposers! Have students research and write a paragraph describing the habitats of their organisms, too.

You can either have students draw directly on the fabric squares or use an ink-jet printer to transfer their diagrams to special iron-on paper. Then ask parents or older mentors to help the students put their quilt together—or trade squares with another school. If you like, auction the quilt at your next school fundraiser and use the money to fund another student project. How about "purchasing" acres in the rain forest or buying seeds and shovels to create a native-pollinator garden or native-habitat area in your school yard?

Meltwater is running water that comes from melted snow or ice. Meltwater moves downhill as the snow or ice melts, supplying freshwater to the places it passes through. But, as the world warms, there is less snow and ice to supply meltwater. Thus many areas

Shown: Stephanie Selznick (holding quilt). Used with permission.

that depend on meltwater from the mountains are experiencing dramatic changes. For example, streams carrying a reduced volume of water carry increased concentrations of nutrients. The nutrients are dumped into wetlands and estuaries and can have dramatic results.

Activity 4.2 asks students to graph real data that show how higher concentrations of nutrients in stream water foster the growth of algae and plants. The data are adapted from a study done at the University of Alaska's Toolik Field Station, the location of the Arctic Long Term Ecological Research, or ARC LTER, site. The full data are posted online at http://tiee.ecoed.net/vol/v3/issues/data_sets/arc/data.html.

• • •

Distribute a copy of Student Sheet 4.2 to each student. Discuss the data set on the student sheet, shown below. Explain that these data are real and part of a set of data obtained by scientists researching the Kuparuk River. The Kuparuk River is a fairly small, clear, and meandering river in the Arctic. Many scientists who work at the ARC LTER are interested in questions related to nutrients brought into the river from its watershed. They study nutrients such as nitrogen (N) and phosphorus (P) by adding them to the river system and watching the effects. The findings of this research apply to many other areas where diminishing freshwater carries increasing concentrations of nutrients.

The data set shows the temperature of the river, measured in degrees Celsius. It also shows the river's flow rate

TABLE 4.2.1 Chlorophyll Comparison in the Kuparuk River

YEAR	AVERAGE WATER TEMP (°C)	AVERAGE RIVER FLOW (M³/CM)	REFERENCE CHLOROPHYLL (μG/CM²)	FERTILIZED CHLOROPHYLL (μG/CM²)
1983		1.2	0.04	2.73
1984		4.0	0.20	0.90
1985	9.0	2.1	0.94	2.23
1986	9.1	2.6	0.35	1.40
1987		3.5	0.16	0.26
1988	8.8	1.3	0.62	8.93
1989	10.5	2.8	0.37	3.31
1990	12.9	0.4	0.49	0.87
1991	9.6	1.7	0.27	1.73
1992	9.8	2.2	0.54	0.64
1993	10.1	2.9	0.13	0.26
1994	10.3	2.7	0.05	0.06
1995	8.8	4.2	0.19	0.36
1996	8.2	2.2	0.16	0.33
1997	9.8	2.8	0.19	0.34
1998	10.9		0.15	0.59

or *discharge,* measured in units of cubic meters per centimeter (m³/cm). (More specifically, discharge is the volume of water that a stream transports in a given time.) Chlorophyll is measured in units of micrograms per square centimeter (µg/cm²). Note that chlorophyll, here, is *epilithic chlorophyll*—a type of chlorophyll in algae that can be scraped from the surface of rocks and other river materials. The reference values of chlorophyll refer to the control data set, whereas the fertilized values reflect data from the portions of the river where the scientists introduced nutrients. Explain to students that the amount of chlorophyll found indicates the amount of algae present.

Questions for Students

1. What factors can affect the flow of an Arctic river?

2. Why do we measure chlorophyll?

3. When scientists added nutrients to the river, how did chlorophyll change?

4. What effects would these changes have on other parts of the food chain?

5. In recent years less snow in the Andes has reduced the water flow to rainforest rivers. River flow slows and some areas become shallow lakes in the dry season. What do data from the Arctic tell us about the potential changes in the Amazon?

● ● ●

FIGURE 4.3.1

SOURCE: NASA/Goddard Space Flight Center. (2014). *Climate Variability—NASA Science*. Retrieved from http://eoimages.gsfc.nasa.gov/images/imagerecords/3000/3394/psn.modis.2002_lrg.jpg.

In addition to surface currents and upwellings, students need to understand *productivity,* or how much photosynthesis is happening. More technically, this is how much carbon dioxide is "fixed" or bound into food molecules. Productivity is color- coded on the map above. For photosynthesis to happen, water, carbon dioxide, and sunlight are necessary, plus some nutrients to help the chemical reactions work. (Nutrients act much like fertilizer.)

Students will need Internet access to do this activity. They will need to interact with the map above, which is posted at http://www .nasa.gov/topics/earth/features/plankton-study.html.

They will also need a little prior knowledge.

Be sure your students know about *surface currents*—wind-driven streams of water that move relative to the larger ocean. Surface currents move in a relatively constant pattern, distributing heat all over the globe by transporting waters far from their source. The Gulf Stream, for example, is a surface current that brings warm equatorial water westward around the Gulf of Mexico and then northward along the eastern coast of the United States. They should also understand *upwellings,* currents that rise from deep water to the surface and often bring nutrients with them.

Students will also need to know that latitude lines are horizontal lines that ring the Earth. *Hint:* If students tend to confuse longitude and latitude, just remind them that "lats are flat." The equator, at latitude 0°, receives maximum sunlight, while the poles, at north or south latitude 90°, receive minimum solar radiation.

To begin the activity, give each student a copy of Student Sheet 4.3. Ask the students to follow the prompts on the sheet to find areas of high productivity. They should come away realizing that productivity in the ocean is linked to available nutrients and that the distribution of nutrients depends on winds and vertical mixing of ocean water, which in turn depend on temperature.

Sample NGSS Crosscutting Concepts

Patterns

- Different patterns may be observed at each of the scales at which a system is studied and can provide evidence for causality in explanations of phenomena. (HS-PS1-1), (HS-PS1-2), (HS-PS-3), (HS-PS1-5)

Energy and Matter

- In nuclear processes, atoms are not conserved, but the total number of protons plus neutrons is conserved. (HS-PS1-8)

- The total amount of energy and matter in closed systems is conserved. (HS-PS1-7)

- Changes of energy and matter in a system can be described in terms of energy and matter flows into, out of, and within that system. (HS-PS1-4)

Stability and Change

- Much of science deals with constructing explanations of how things change and how they remain stable. (HS-PS1-6)

5

Felix

Plants for the Planet

Activities in This Chapter:

Activity 5.1. Bird's-Eye Ecology

Activity 5.2. Plant for the Planet—and for Our Future

Take a virtual tour of the Earth. Ride on Google Earth or NASA satellites. What is the state of Earth's green carpet of vegetation, which is so vital to life?

There might have been a time when most of the places you flew over were green. Not so today. Human structures, desertification, and deforestation have changed many areas. The Earthshots website has collections of time-lapse photography of natural areas over decades that illustrate how anthropogenic (human-generated) action has affected ecosystems.

The most dramatic observations relate to deforestation. It's easy to demonstrate that trees—the "lungs of the planet"—are vital for our future. And it's easy to find vast areas where forests are disappearing. Desertification is a phenomenon that is threatening Africa, the Caribbean, the western United States, and vast parts of Asia. When it occurs, it quickly affects human survival in the most basic ways.

In Germany, fourth grader Felix Finkbeiner had a dream. It started when he studied the value of trees in school. He had been inspired by the work of (2004) Nobel Peace Prize winner Wangari Maathai, who created the Green Belt Movement—a tree-planting campaign in Kenya. In January 2007 he finished his fourth-grade class presentation with these words: "Let's plant millions of trees worldwide—a million in each country!" The student initiative Plant-for-the-Planet was born.

His message was simple: "Stop talking, start planting." Coordinated by Felix's efforts, students in Germany had already planted one million trees by the end of 2009. His website, at http://www.plant-for-the-planet.org, connected young people all over the world. The site encouraged donations and coordinated planting. Felix enlisted celebrities and heads of state such as Prince Albert of Monaco to spread word of his tree-planting efforts. The Billion Tree Campaign, a vast tree-planting program overseen by the United Nations Environment Programme (UNEP), exceeded its goal by planting 12 billion trees by 2011. Later that year, UNEP honored Felix by handing over the Billion Tree Campaign to Plant-for-the-Planet, giving Felix even more resources to work with as well as great responsibility. At the time this book was going to press, Felix's website counter for trees planted worldwide had reached almost 13 billion!

It's hard to imagine accomplishing as much as Felix did in just four years. A single tree can fix (use) 48 pounds (21.8 kg) of carbon a day. Each person in the United States generates approximately 2.3 tons

(2,087 kg) of CO_2 each year. A healthy tree stores about 13 pounds (5.9 kg) of carbon annually—or 2.6 tons (2,359 kg) per acre. Of course, most of the trees planted through Felix's efforts are still small. But you do the math! Or you can download software to estimate the carbon use of trees of various sizes and ages from the U.S. Forest Service's Climate Change Resource Center at http://www.fs.fed.us/ccrc/topics/urban-forests/ctcc.

Felix Finkbeiner
Plant for the Planet

This activity integrates math with ecology and technology. It is based on the U.S. Geological Survey's Earthshots website at http://earthshots.usgs.gov/earthshots. The site features satellite images taken of the same regions over time, revealing the extent of environmental change. In this exercise, students look at satellite photos and use a grid technique to estimate the percentage of the land that has been altered.

Figure 5.1.1 shows deforestation in Haiti. Figures 5.1.2a and 5.1.2b show development in the vicinity of Disney World in Orlando, Florida, occurring between 1973 and 2011.

Distribute a copy of Student Sheet 5.1 to each student. While students are doing estimations, they should be able to calculate that Haiti (in this area) is less than 10 percent forested, while the Dominican Republic is about 70 percent forested. In the images of Disney World, about 25 percent of the green space was lost in the process of development.

The green carpet of plant life covering much of Earth is diminishing. This affects life in so many ways! The bottom level of most food pyramids is composed of photosynthesizers. And, of course, plants and other photosynthesizing organisms play a crucial role in atmospheric chemistry, for they consume

FIGURE 5.1.1

SOURCE: NASA/Goddard Space Flight Center. (2014). *SVS Animation 2640—Haitian Deforestation.* Retrieved from http://commons.wikimedia.org/wiki/File:Haiti_deforestation.jpg.

FIGURE 5.1.2A Orlando, Florida, USA (1973)   **FIGURE 5.1.2B** Orlando, Florida, USA (2011)

SOURCE: U.S. Geological Survey. (2014). *Earthshots: Satellite Images of Environmental Change.* Retrieved from http://earthshots.usgs.gov/earthshots/node/47#ad-image-0.

carbon dioxide and release molecular oxygen. Activity 5.2 gives kids a chance to look at the relationship between plants and the organisms that consume them quantitatively.

This activity is a thought experiment that parallels a hands-on activity. It asks the students to imagine that they create a closed habitat in a soda bottle with plants and animals. They calculate the oxygen consumed and the carbon dioxide produced by their model ecosystem and reflect on how much plant life is needed to sustain it. Hand each student a copy of Student Sheet 5.2 to get started. No other materials or resources are required.

Sample NGSS Disciplinary Core Idea

MS-LS2-3: Ecosystems: Interactions, Energy, and Dynamics

- Develop a model to describe the cycling of matter and flow of energy among living and nonliving parts of an ecosystem.

6 Green Ambassadors

Activities in This Chapter:

In today's global community, projects can stretch across states, countries, and continents. Many times, powerful global efforts begin small—as small as a single seed. That's what the Green Ambassadors did. Working together, they planted fruit trees.

Through the energy of one community's youth, a transformation has occurred. The Green Ambassadors don't just plant trees, they also educate their younger peers. In that way, they perpetuate the good they do for "their sisters' kids, and their kids' kids." (Green Ambassadors Institute is a learning lab project of the Environmental Charter School program of the University of California, Los Angeles, and is supported by UCLA Extension. Learn more at http://greenambassadors.org.)

Similarly, Activity 6.1—which involves surveying the air in the community for pollutants—can be part of a big and "crowd-sourced" project.

The world is changing, and fast. Activity 6.2 will help everyone—your young students and the older people with whom they will be working—appreciate the pace of change.

The Green Ambassadors are great communicators about the climate crisis. Igniting public interest in climate conservation can take a bit of salesmanship! Activity 6.3 will help your students learn how to communicate this issue in a convincing way, just as the Green Ambassadors have been able to do.

Many times we move through our daily routines without noticing the changes in the environment around us. This is especially true with subtle changes like air pollution.

Provide students with standard lengths (3 cm) of white, double-sided tape (such as the kind you might use to hold down a carpet). Make a label for each piece of tape by sticking a small piece of paper to one end. Mark one side of the paper "Top" and the other side "Bottom." Place these pieces of tape, top side exposed to the air, at specific sites around your community—near roads, behind buildings, in fields and forested areas. After three to five days, collect them and immediately protect them by sliding each one into a snack baggie. Label each snack baggie with the test site location.

Have students examine each piece of tape under a magnifying glass. Count how many particles are on each piece of tape. For each piece of tape, also qualitatively describe the particulates that were collected. What color are the particles? How big are they?

Prepare a poster-size or larger map of your community that includes the test sites. Mount the tape samples on the map to illustrate the air pollution in various areas. Also, record the number of particles collected per centimeter of tape on the map so that particulate pollution levels at different sites can be compared.

Ask students, "If you were going to have a picnic, what would be the most favorable location in terms of particulate air pollution?"

Also, be sure to mention that air pollution comes in various forms, including emitted gases such as carbon dioxide and ozone as well as suspended particles—particulates. Particulates exhausted into the air are mostly carbon that comes from the combustion of fuels. Just as natural particulates, including pollen, may be irritating, so may human-produced particulates. Prolonged exposure to human-produced particulates can result in chronic health conditions including cancer and damage to the body's immune, neurological, reproductive, and respiratory systems. People with asthma, kids, and the elderly are the groups most susceptible to such effects.

● ● ●

Collect photos of your community "then and now" showing the changes in areas like "Main Street" over 100 years.

Combine these with the data collected on air pollution, aerial photographs of tree cover, and podcasts in which senior citizens talk about the changes on a more personal basis.

You can do this activity in a public location, creating a mural or diorama to which many people can contribute. Or you can create a Wiki site where community participation can be created in a virtual space.

For inspiration, see how the Woods Hole Research Center represents land-use changes in Cape Cod since 1951 at http://www.whrc.org/mapping/capecod. Show your students the map with the slider; they will be astonished to see how much forest has been converted to residential space in less than sixty years. Click the "Losing Cape Cod" button to see graphic displays of projected climate change impacts on Cape Cod. These displays make it clear that human population growth affects the environment and climate in particular. Also, check out another great mapping technique for showing then-and-now land-use data from the Woods Hole Research Center at http://www.whrc.org/mapping/capecod/landcoveroverview.html.

• • •

This activity asks students to play the role of a tree salesperson going door-to-door. They use facts about trees to write "sales pitches" for their imaginary customers. They imagine the responses as well. All in all, this is an exercise that prepares students to hold intelligent and persuasive conversations about the benefits of trees to the climate. Give each student a copy of Student Sheet 6.3 and get started! This activity can easily be done in pairs. The kids can share their sales pitches with partners, compare real responses to imagined responses, and then use the feedback to hone their sales pitches.

• • •

STANDARDS

Sample NGSS Disciplinary Core Ideas

LS2.A: Interdependent Relationships in Ecosystems

- The food of almost any kind of animal can be traced back to plants. Organisms are related in food webs in which some animals eat plants for food and other animals eat the animals that eat plants. Some organisms, such as fungi and bacteria, break down dead organisms (both plants or plant parts and animals) and therefore operate as "decomposers." Decomposition eventually restores (recycles) some materials back to the soil. Organisms can survive only in environments in which their particular needs are met. A healthy ecosystem is one in which multiple species of different types are each able to meet their needs in a relatively stable web of life. Newly introduced species can damage the balance of an ecosystem. (5-LS2-1)

Sample Common Core Standard

CCSS.ELA-Literacy.WHST.6–8.1b. Support claim(s) with logical reasoning and relevant, accurate data and evidence that demonstrate an understanding of the topic or text, using credible sources.

7 Dreaming in Green

Activity in This Chapter:

George Washington Carver Middle School in Coral Gables, Florida, is a typical school in many ways—great teachers, enthusiastic learners, dynamic athletic teams. (Go Cougars!) Bertha Vazquez has been teaching her students at Carver to read critically and research their sources for two decades.

Research is a basic skill at Carver. Students find out facts and think for themselves. In Mrs. Vazquez's science classes, the students begin by researching the credibility of various sources on climate change. This essential process of science gives students a foundation of process skills and a healthy dose of skepticism about the media. Bertha's curriculum has produced students who not only inquire and investigate but also now are "Dreaming in Green." Dream in Green is a nonprofit organization that develops programs to promote environmental sustainability. It conducts the Green Schools Challenge, a program that provides resources for students who are motivated to do something for the planet. Carver's Green Team took the opportunity and ran with it!

The target of Carver's Green Team was energy use. Students discovered that their school was wasting enormous amounts of energy and money. They didn't stop there, though. When those same students looked for a way to act, they developed a project that was not only practical but also profitable. They conducted an energy audit of Carver Middle School and presented their recommendations to the administration and the board. The result: thousands of dollars in savings each year. The idea spread, and now those same students are using their "can-do" attitude to make changes at the district's high schools.

One of the most impressive aspects of the Green Team's success was the ease with which the students were able to convince the reluctant decision makers in their school community to become more energy conscious. The key was the money savings that energy stewardship could produce. The kids' energy recommendations reduced not only their school's carbon footprint but its overhead too! As the members of the first Green Team moved into secondary school they found it easy to recruit more adult advocates for their energy audit recommendations.

Activity 7.1 is a Web quest loosely adapted from ideas that have been outstandingly successful for the students in Bertha Vazquez's science classes at Carver Middle School.

Students work in pairs to do Internet research to discover the various ways that climate change is being represented in the media. Give each student a copy of Student Sheet 7.1. The sheet provides instructions on doing a Web search on the topic of climate change. Students try different key words, compare hits, and disregard sites that can be identified as biased. That is, students learn to eliminate particular kinds of sites:

- Sites that are commercial
- "Secondary" sources (opinion articles and blog sites)
- Commercial sites that are sponsored by companies

Students then screen their remaining sites by checking on the organizations and "experts" behind the sites. They use questions such as the following:

- Who is the author? Is she or he a scientist or a journalist?
- If the author is a scientist, does she or he have a reputation in the scientific world? Is she or he employed by a commercial firm? If the scientist has a website, who supports her or his research?
- Where does the funding come from? Who donates to the organization? Do donors have political or commercial affiliations?
- Where do the scientists publish? Do they publish in peer-reviewed journals? What is a peer-reviewed journal, and how is publishing in one different from publishing in a magazine or a blog?

FIGURE 7.1.1

Image used with permission.

This same sort of research can be done in regard to many of the "experts" who are featured on cable television news shows. Many viewers have contacted various media outlets to request that all of the potential affiliations and conflicts of interest of the commentators they feature be made public.

• • •

Sample Common Core Standard

CCSS.ELA-Literacy.RST.6-8.1

- Cite specific textual evidence to support analysis of science and technical texts.

Sample NGSS Disciplinary Core Idea

Practices of Science: Argumentation (6-8)

- Compare and critique two arguments on the same topic and analyze whether they emphasize similar or different evidence and/or interpretations of facts.

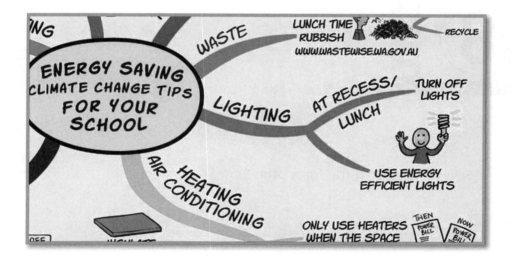

8 Olivia's Birds

Olivia Bouler loves birds. She came to know them by careful observation each day. So when the oil rig *Deepwater Horizon* exploded and oil flooded the beaches of the Gulf of Mexico, she knew that her birds would be in very serious trouble.

Everyone has talents. One of Olivia's great talents is drawing. So she offered her art skill to produce drawings that could be sold to help fund efforts to clean the oiled birds of the Gulf of Mexico. Her work caught the attention of the media—and the world. Eventually Olivia raised $200,000 for the Audubon Society's efforts to wash the oil off the birds. In 2011, she authored and illustrated the inspiring children's book *Olivia's Birds: Saving the Gulf.* Olivia's example is one that students all over the world can emulate. Take what you have, act locally—and have global impact.

Because, as Olivia says, birds "rule the air" and often migrate across large expanses of continents, they are particularly sensitive to the changes that are occurring in Earth's climate. In Activity 8.1, students explore the effects of climate change on one small and endangered species—the Kirtland's warbler. Then they explore the adaptations of birds and how they might be affected by changes in habitat.

Give each student a copy of Student Sheet 8.1. Students will read the following paragraphs and engage with some critical thinking questions afterward.

Each spring the lengthening days send a message to a little bird—the Kirtland's warbler—on the islands of the Caribbean: "Fly north. Find exactly the right spot to make a nest and nurture a new generation." That place is a few hundred acres in northern Michigan near the city of Grayling, where the jack pine trees are just the right height and the sandy soil is exactly what the birds prefer. The birds' sun calendar brings them to those specific trees just in time to find hatching caterpillars, food for their own hatchlings.

Two threats caused the Kirtland population to dwindle almost to extinction: humans cut down many of the trees and changed the habitat, and birds of another species—cowbirds—often snuck their own eggs into the warblers' nests. Since cowbird eggs hatch more quickly than warbler eggs, the newly hatched cowbirds got most of the tasty caterpillars and the new warbler babies starved. (The story of the effect of cowbirds on another migratory bird species, the wood thrush, can be found in Lynne Cherry's book *Flute's Journey: The Life of a Wood Thrush.*)

A massive effort to save the Kirtland's warbler had a lot of success. People realized that the jack pine forests had to be protected. The population began to grow again.

But in recent years, something changed. The average temperature of the northern forests is increasing. (Remember, birds are homeothermic, or warm-blooded, while insects like caterpillars are ectothermic, sometimes called cold-blooded.) Think about how this might affect the life cycles of birds and insects.

FIGURE 8.1.1 Migratory Route for the Kirtland's Warbler

This activity can be done in a think-pair-share format, each student working with a partner. You can follow up this activity with a discussion of other species that are endangered because their habitats are changing under climate change. For example, investigate the Edith's checkerspot butterfly, the polar bear, or the orangutan. Information on these and other endangered species can be found in *How We Know What We Know About Our Changing Climate,* by Lynne Cherry and Gary Braasch.

. . .

STANDARDS

NGSS Disciplinary Core Idea

LS2.C: Ecosystem Dynamics, Functioning, and Resilience

- When the environment changes in ways that affect a place's physical characteristics, temperature, or availability of resources, some organisms survive and reproduce, others move to new locations, yet others move into the transformed environment, and some die. (secondary to 3-LS4-4)

Sample Common Core Standard

CCSS.ELA-Literacy.RST.6-8.7

- Integrate quantitative or technical information expressed in words in a text with a version of that information expressed visually (e.g., in a flowchart, diagram, model, graph, or table).

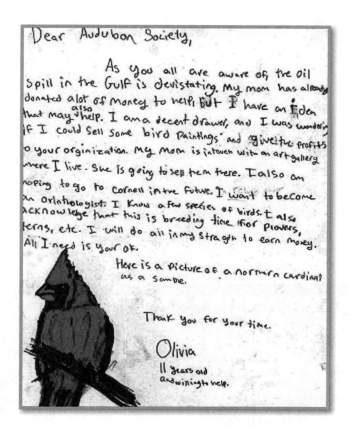

Dear Audubon Society,

As you all are aware of, the oil spill in the Gulf is devistating. My mom has already donated a lot of money to help, but I have an idea also that may help. I am a decent drawer, and I was wondering if I could sell some 'bird paintings' and give the profits to your orginization. My mom is intouch with an art gallery where I live. She is going to sell them there. I also am hoping to go to Cornell in the future. I want to become an ornithologist. I know a few species of birds. I also acknowledge that this is breeding time for plovers, terns, etc. I will do all in my stragth to earn money. All I need is your ok.

Here is a picture of a northern cardinal as a sample.

Thank you for your time.

Olivia
11 years old
and wining to help.

9

Longing for a Local Lunch

Activities in This Chapter:

There was a time—the first million years or so of human existence—when what was for dinner depended on the season and where you happened to be. Today in much of the world you can buy almost any kind of food at almost any time of the year. American food items travel an average of 1,500 to 2,500 miles (2,414 to 4,023 km) from farm to table. Even if you live in Iowa, the center of the nation's agriculture, there's a good chance the tomatoes in your supermarket have traveled 1,500 miles (2,414 km) from where they were grown.

But what is the cost of all that travel? If you crave fresh carrots in June or fresh tomatoes in December, should you buy them? How do the carbon footprints and the nutritional value of out-of-season vegetables compare with those of the vegetables you buy from local sources in season? These are questions we rarely ask!

In one high school, students did ask these questions. They found surprising answers and interesting solutions for their school community. The film *Longing for a Local Lunch* tells the story of how these students from Great Barrington, Massachusetts, were able to eat local. They grew some of their own food in their school garden. But since the most productive season was summer, they traded their summer produce for vegetables from the local co-op in the fall and winter, when they couldn't grow their own. By bartering, they ended up with a more nutritious, less expensive school menu that released far less carbon into the planet's atmosphere.

To understand the problem of our long-distance food supply and the solution, students must begin by shopping.

Activity 9.2 will help kids understand that local, healthy food was the norm for people until very recently.

Awaken the critical consumer in your students with Activity 9.3. Students will find out how far the food in their local grocery stores has traveled. They will ponder both the nutritional and energy costs involved in shipping food long distances.

If you and your students are hungry for delicious local food after watching *Longing for a Local Lunch,* realize that you can grow good nutritious food wherever you may be located. Activity 9.4 will guide your inquiry into the possibility of starting a school garden.

Despite our ability to move food across the globe, many American inner cities have been described as "food deserts." It is almost impossible for people who live in some of these neighborhoods to gain access to fresh and affordable fruits and vegetables.

The Urban EcoLab Curriculum includes an outline for a lesson in which students investigate food deserts. See http://urbanecolabcurriculum.com/modules/module-5/module-5-lesson-6-income-and-food-options.

The EcoLab Curriculum also includes a lesson in calculating the distance your food travels. See http://urbanecolab curriculum.com/modules/module-3/module-3-lesson-6-food-choices-and-climate-change.

Food creates strong memories in most people. Find the oldest members of your community. Ask them to record podcasts in which they describe what they ate and where they got their food when they were young. Ask them if they grew their own. Ask them about "victory gardens."

Are those same food sources available today?

Take your students to a nearby grocery store. Or if this is not convenient, bring grocery store items to class. Students will examine labels to see where each food item was produced. They will then use a map or an Internet search engine to calculate how many miles the product traveled. One online resource that will help them is the City Distance Tool offered on the Geobytes website at http://www.geobytes.com/citydistancetool.htm.

Give each student a copy of Student Sheet 9.3. Students can organize their findings by filling in the chart on the worksheet.

Distribute Student Sheet 9.4 to the students. Use it to frame your discussion. The first topic to discuss will be what kinds of edible plants grow in your region. Students are guided to consider the space, light, temperature, and growing-time requirements of various options.

A chart showing what plants grow where will help them. Also, they are guided to this online information source for more help figuring out what to grow: http://www.nass.usda.gov/Publications/Usual_Planting_and_Harvesting_Dates/uph97.pdf.

Finally, students will plan what to grow. They will make a calendar with harvest times so that they will have fresh food all year.

• • •

Make a community cookbook that features local foods in season:

- Late carrots in the fall
- Early asparagus in the spring

Use your cookbook or cooking website to educate.

• • •

STANDARDS

Notes

PART

Make It Happen in a Community Near You!

Part I of this book is all about energy—the unharnessed power of young people who believe in themselves and the future of Earth. You've read about and viewed examples of model projects and outstanding accomplishments.

This second part of the book is about inertia. As any teacher can understand, it's sometimes hard for young people to get started. But once they are in motion, watch out! The tips and cautions in this section are meant to be practical guides to get the youth you work with started and moving steadily toward their own goals.

TILLING THE SOIL

The most effective student projects begin with authentic student ideas. But as in most fruitful gardens, first the soil must be enriched! Students have to feel that their environment is safe for exploration—of both the natural world and ideas that can improve it. That requires that they trust the adults in their learning communities to have both open minds and a sense of humor. The worst "herbicide" in a garden of blooming ideas is an attitude that says, "That's not possible."

The second requirement for nurturing good ideas is a set of tools. Remember the example of Bertha Vazquez at Carver Middle School in Florida. Her students didn't walk in the door with a healthy skepticism about media reports on climate change. They developed that skepticism by learning and using sound research skills. Mrs. Vazquez's lessons in critical thinking taught students to question and investigate. When they came up with answers, they were all the more prepared to argue their case to school and community. In most instances, such preparation is going to require that students learn about how their local communities are governed and serviced. Where does the water come from? How do you get a permit to meet? Whom do you call if you want to speak at a town meeting? Who is responsible for making sure something happens or doesn't happen?

The third element is content knowledge. It was the knowledge of photosynthesis, carbon sequestration, and the value of trees to mitigate climate change that sparked German student Felix Finkbeiner to plant trees. From Felix's understanding of the basic biology that helps balance the planet's atmosphere came his simple yet powerful plan: plant trees—not just a few but a lot. His challenge to the youth of his generation began with this scientific knowledge. One young voice called and millions answered.

Establishing a curriculum that provides a sound science content foundation *and* encourages students to think isn't easy, especially in an atmosphere where scores on tests often overwhelm everything else. But it can be done. Scan the activities in Part I of this book. The activities described there are clearly related to one or more national standards. This set of links to standards isn't meant to be comprehensive, but rather suggestive.

What if your mentoring responsibilities aren't in a classroom, but in a less formal setting, like a club or youth center? In many ways, it's easier to nurture young scientist/activists when their initial ideas start from academic lessons, but that's not a necessary element. In a club, extracurricular, or independent effort, the basic science that the "movers and shakers" will need can be provided *on the fly*. Students quickly realize that in order to create effective public relations campaigns or sway their local city council, they need to know real facts and how to communicate. As Larissa Weinstein says in *Dreaming in Green*, "We were taken seriously because we had real statistics and information." The vital scientific practice of *argumentation*, which is discussed prominently in the Next Generation Science Standards, is one of the key skills that young voices need today.

The message here is clear. In the open air, in the warmth of the sun and a warm community, your young voices can bloom, grow, and produce wonderful crops!

FINDING A NICHE

Many people associate the sorts of projects we've seen motivating students' conduct—and those you might brainstorm with your own class—with the traditional idea of a "science club." That's certainly a format that works in some schools and communities. But it's not necessary for the activities to fall under the organizational structure of a club or extracurricular activity. The main reason teachers give for pushing the really motivational activities outside the five-hour school day is the pressure of the formal curriculum. In those circumstances, the requirements of the program or the test sometimes encourage inertia. But they need not; the NGSS can actually encourage action.

> There are powerful arguments for integrating activism into the regular school day.

Activist projects can be the basis of project-based learning. And as you doubtless have heard, much research demonstrates the effectiveness of project-based learning. Projects can be closely aligned with national and state objectives. They require reading, writing, communicating, measurement, and other mathematics skills. Most important, they teach these skills in a way that always answers the question "Why do we have to learn this?" It's easy to find evidence in the literature that students who tackle projects that grab their minds and hearts are more likely to *want* to learn the basic content of their courses.

There are ways to structure a class project that don't sap inordinate amounts of time from the school day—at least at first. Asking students to research the steps that would be necessary to achieve a project can become a valuable assignment. Parents can become involved by helping students interview community stakeholders or explore sites for their work as part of a social studies unit. School media personnel, administrators, and even noninstructional facilities staff are often very excited about the possibility of getting involved. Many hands make light work.

Embedding a community project into the curriculum of a given grade or grade span has other advantages, too. It can quickly become part of the school tradition. ("Fourth graders measure the water quality in our river" or "Sixth grade is the year we record the migration of butterflies.") This sort of ongoing activism and the maintenance of records and exhibits fall nicely into the role of a media center and become a great source of school pride.

But don't be surprised if the project that fits nicely into an integrated curriculum at first eventually becomes too big for a standard class period. Remember inertia? An object in motion remains in motion! Then the places in which budding citizen science can flourish may be limited only by the imagination. Consider these options:

- "Latchkey" activities—structured time that extends the school day
- After-school enrichment—voluntary groups that students join to explore and accomplish mutual goals

- Summer school science—project-based programs to encourage careers or achievement
- In-school enrichment sections—opportunities for gifted students to go beyond the curriculum
- Remedial sections—projects interwoven with basic skills in a seamless way
- Homeschool networks—opportunities for students to interact and cooperate
- Outside groups—Scouts, 4H, church or community groups, veterans' or other military groups

Many of the organizational tips and cautions in the sections that follow presume that student activism will happen outside the standard class period. Such club or club-like structures carry some inherent risks, and forethought is especially important for them. But the requirement of appropriate caution should not prevent a group from moving outside the school yard. It is just one more factor to consider as students plan.

MAKING IT HAPPEN

One evening after a long lecture on climate change, an eighteen-year-old student challenged one of the authors. "I make minimum wage. One day a week I work just to fill my gas tank. What can someone like me do about global warming?" That was the opening! With mouse in hand, the instructor pulled up *Team Marine,* a video of the campaign to ban plastic bags in Santa Monica. Like the students in California, the students in this class lived by the ocean and had often seen the damage done by plastic to sea animals and the environment. But they had never been personally challenged to take a step themselves. Inspired by Team Marine, the skeptical student and the entire class left buzzing. There was *something* they could do! It wasn't an impossible dream; in fact, it was as near as their local grocery store. From that single question a student club evolved.

Those sorts of moments occur in every group and every class. The conversation might take place in the school commons, on a bus, or in a coffee shop. It often happens when the activities that the adult facilitator had planned begin to get dull or seem to be leading to dead ends. Science "clubs" can tire of packaged experiments or guest speakers; youth groups can run out of badges or certificates to earn.

When an authentic idea pops up, don't let the energy dissipate. Grab a piece of chalk, a marker, or a keyboard. Ask an open question: Is there something we could do about it? Then give the questioner(s) time. That's the best sort of mentoring. Make a list of ideas. No idea is too crazy or impractical at this point. Let the dust settle and the marker ink dry. But don't file that list! Come back to it the next day and ask those who generated it to categorize their ideas: impractical, inconsequential, . . . or *possible*. That column contains the gold.

After some time, reconstruct that chart by adding four more columns: What would it take? Who would have to help? Where would you begin? What's the first step? Cross out ideas that are clearly impossible or unsafe, but challenge your students to think of alternatives to those dead ends. When you hit a wall, walk around it.

Another of this book's authors showed the *Young Voices for the Planet* films to her friend's three daughters. Afterward, nine-year-old Alice Van Evera, clearly revved up, grabbed her notebook and a pencil and said, "We have to do something! I'm not sure what . . . but I'm going to start a club. We'll call it . . . 'Saving Tomorrow'!" One month later, the middle school members of Saving Tomorrow testified at the town meeting in Lexington, Massachusetts, asking to repeal a law preventing solar panels from being mounted on public buildings. They got a standing ovation, the law was repealed, and now solar panels are being put on town buildings.

Through a formal evaluation of the films, we found that in a matter of minutes, they can transform young people from feeling hopeless to hopeful and from feeling powerless to believing that they—kids—can make a difference. As Alec Loorz says in *Kids vs Global Warming,* "Kids have power!"

FOSTERING TEAMWORK AMONG DIVERSE LEARNERS WITH UNIQUE SKILLS

When a group articulates a plan, there are usually those who rise up to lead and those who are reluctant to get involved. It's important for kids to realize that any group project will require a wide variety of skills. Your role as mentor will involve being sensitive not just to those who "drive the train" but also to those who prefer to be "the caboose." Do what you can to foster a climate of collective action, mutual respect, and inclusiveness. One way to do this is to teach your young activists some cooperative games. The game below is an example. You can find many more at CooperativeGames.com, a website created by one of the authors of this book.

You will need a soda can. It will serve as an imaginary container of "toxic waste." Have your group form a circle with participants about a foot apart. Explain that the group goal is to pass the can around the circle without anyone using their hands or dropping the can. Ew! Get rid of it but don't drop it!

When you finish playing any cooperative game, reflect on it as a group to promote healthy group dynamics. Ask questions such as: Was the game fun? Did we achieve our goal? Did everyone try their best? Were all group members kind and helpful to anyone who struggled with the task? How is playing this game like working together on a climate preservation project?

You'll want to be especially sensitive to students who might be hesitant to participate for cultural or socioeconomic reasons:

- Do you have students whose transportation is limited because of lack of auto transport?

- Do you have students who might be reluctant to be involved in local government because of citizenship issues?

- Do you have students who might not be able to get to the beach, the forest, or the wetlands because of handicapping conditions or allergies?

- Do you have students whose parents might be suspicious of their children's participation because of political, cultural, or religious perspectives?

- If you will be fundraising, do you have students who can't participate for financial reasons or because their neighborhoods aren't safe for soliciting?

Encourage students to come forward and try to find work-arounds so that your project is equal opportunity and reflects the entire community. Better yet, be sure that students from marginalized groups have voices in structuring the project. They will design projects that are meaningful to their own communities and doable by community members.

POLISHING THE PLAN

Many student groups have highly energetic starts, then stall. The first few meetings involve great thoughts, great synergy—and then the enormity of the challenge hits the group. What, after all, can we do that could actually make a difference? It all seems too big. The adults we've consulted are too skeptical. The bureaucracy is too thick. Someone tried that before and it didn't work.

To return to the analogy of inertia, those excuses are like friction. Once a group of energetic young people has formed, it's important to "grease the skids" to keep the wheels rolling. A mentor can identify at least one concrete step that can be taken—one with measurable results.

It's important to think about time here. Psychologists talk about people's sense of "fate control"—how far into the future a goal can seem within reach. In general, young people need shorter timelines for results. Changing the CO_2 level in the atmosphere is a huge, decades-long goal. Changing an international treaty or even a state or local law may take years. These are all great goals, but young people need to see shorter-term success to feel empowered. That means a project with real results in real time.

Projects that have worked for other groups include the following:

- Action projects to reduce CO_2 emissions in local, measurable settings. For example:
  - Using less energy in homes, school, or transportation
  - Reducing use of products made from fossil fuels in the community
  - Distributing products that use less energy, such as metal water canteens ("clean canteens"), cloth shopping bags, or CFL or LED lightbulbs

- "Green" projects. For example:
  - Planting green spaces
  - Remodeling roofs or other areas of campus
  - Planting school gardens
  - Getting a fraction of the school's energy from renewable sources

- Education projects focusing on climate change–related topics. For example:
  - How to conserve energy at school through an energy audit
  - The cumulative effects of small actions by individuals
  - The long-term effects of short-term carelessness

- Media projects: podcasts, PowerPoint presentations, or films to change attitudes in the community regarding climate change–related issues. For example:
  - Using native plants to reduce water consumption
  - Consuming local foods to reduce transportation energy
  - Reusing, repairing, and recycling products
  - Eliminating the use of plastic drinking straws by local restaurants
  - Measuring the amount of carbon monoxide in the classroom before and after school buses idle outside the school or lawn crews use noisy weed whackers or leaf blowers
  - Eliminating pollution caused by school buses idling or the use of weed whackers and leaf blowers
  - Stopping the use of Styrofoam lunch trays and other throwaways at the school
  - Biking to school instead of having parents drive

RECRUITMENT

The maxim might be stretched: "Two's company, three's a movement!" When a few students have a great idea, it's not normally a challenge to get a few more involved. But sometimes the greater challenge is to get the *right* students involved—not just the science types, but a broad spectrum of students. Student groups that reach across the school community are often far more successful in the long run. This is a challenge that is best faced at the very beginning and one in which a wise mentor can have a lot of influence. "Great idea—but we don't just need science here. We need some good artists, some tech-savvy video makers, some students who know how to talk fast to communicate ideas. . . . How do we get them?" If your project, club, or extracurricular activity develops recruiting materials, use the widest possible appeal. Tweeting, rapping, and graphic novel style may not be your first instincts, but they might be near and dear to some highly energetic recruits. Use them!

It's also important to be broad-minded! Students who are sometimes unsuccessful or downright troublesome in the normal school day can be amazingly successful in an outside-school organization. Here they can think outside the box, experience pride, show leadership, and express themselves! You'll need some behavioral guidelines, of course (see below), but don't limit your recruitment by preconceptions.

The second challenge is to get students to *stay involved*. Many groups attract big crowds to the first few meetings, then attendance dwindles. When the real (and often tedious) work of making flyers, stuffing envelopes, or picking up litter begins, sometimes the crowd thins. To maintain enthusiasm, set a clear timeline. Create a visual record of what's been accomplished and what's left to do. (Those graphic "thermometer" graphs aren't just for fundraising.) Set up mile markers for partial success and plan a celebration for each segment of the overall plan. The ultimate criterion for success might be banning bags or seeing a thousand trees blossom, but the first success marker might be a meeting with local elected officials or the Chamber of Commerce or Rotary.

And don't forget visuals. Wristbands and T-shirts are inexpensive reminders that an idea has support. Green tape on the mailboxes of families who are participating in a recycling or planting project can create a powerful subconscious message for an entire community. But as your group plans these efforts, don't forget to be conscious of the impacts. Papering hundreds of cars with flyers is pollution! And plastic wristbands and latex balloons pose great dangers for ocean life. If your publicity materials can be created from recyclables, that's a step forward. If they can be reused or repurposed, all the better.

RECRUITING SUPPORT FROM ABOVE

As soon as an idea reaches the point where students are brainstorming actual plans for a project or club—or even sooner—share those ideas with your administrator. You can do it in a casual way, but remember that forewarned is fore-calmed! Educate yourself about school policies and procedures, local regulations, and community standards.

Consider the rest of the staff as well. We've mentioned media professionals. But staff members in other disciplines who might be very willing to help in the best of circumstances can become very resistant if they aren't informed early about what's happening. If you move ahead alone, you might cause unnecessary friction or competition among staff members when a synergy might have been possible. (You may even want to consider the name of your group or project. The "Science Club" might attract more support in some schools if it is called the "Planet Club." Why should "science" have all the fun and great press?)

Think about the structure of your students' families. Are some very supportive and some very hard to reach? Is there a divide between students with lots of resources and those who have less? Share your students' ideas, from seed to sprout, with the families. Gather their input and their help. And make sure that your communications offer concrete suggestions for small things that almost every family can do. Ask for all kinds of little things, from cookies to recycling bins to brooms and buckets.

ICEBREAKER ACTIVITY: GETTING TO KNOW YOU!

A Think-Pair-Share for Potential Club Members

Everyone has opinions. Yours matter! In this group, everyone's ideas will be respected.

Take a look at each of the situations in the first column of the table below. In the second column, write down your first reaction. Then turn to a person near you. Introduce yourself and discuss your responses. In the third column, write down one thing you and your new friend can agree on about each situation.

SITUATION	YOUR VIEW	SOMETHING WE AGREE ON
Students in your school buy a lot of bottles of water from a vending machine in the hall. A local ecology group wants to donate a refillable metal bottle to each student in the school, but the money from the water vending machine goes to the school's sports teams. Should your school give up plastic bottles?		
A lot of food goes to waste in your school cafeteria. A group has suggested that the cafeteria get rid of trays. That would mean you could take only the food that fits on your plate, and then you'd have to go back to get a new plate if you wanted more. Do you like this idea?		
Your city council is considering a statute that would ban plastic bags at grocery stores. Customers would have to bring their own reusable cloth bags. This might discourage shoppers from out of town, who might not come prepared for the new rules. Would you ask your council to pass the statute?		
The county road commission is thinking about designating some highway lanes as high-occupancy vehicle (HOV) lanes. Only cars with more than one passenger could drive in them. That would make the other lanes much more crowded. Should the commission institute the HOV lanes?		

Now discuss the following question with your partner: When people have very different opinions, how can they have good conversations and get along?

EMPOWERING YOUNG VOICES FOR THE PLANET

Whether your students are concerned about your community's storm drains, the path of trash, or the energy use of vehicles, ask parents to join in the conversation early and often. Pop some corn for a family video night. Make it clear that the parents who show up won't be obligated to assume any big responsibilities (financial or otherwise) at first, so that parents who aren't traditionally involved in school projects realize that it would be easy and low-stress to help.

This is especially important if some of your students come from homes where English is a second language. Is there a part of your project where they have special value? Translating signage? Arranging time at an apartment clubhouse or a local library? Collecting bilingual materials or providing maps? When you can recruit reluctant families, you enrich your efforts.

TOO MUCH MOMENTUM CAN BE INTIMIDATING!

Teachers experience it every day, but to many in business and government the idea of a crowd of enthusiastic middle schoolers invading their offices might be disconcerting. Consider the outside agencies and organizations with which students will have to work to accomplish their goals. How can they best be reached?

While adult mentors shouldn't do the work for youth, there is a lot they can do to smooth students' paths. A phone call or a cup of coffee might be all it takes to turn a potentially confrontational situation into a positive meeting. "My students have some interesting data about the wildlife in the path of your proposed highway expansion. Would you like to see them?" or "A group of students are planning to attend the county board meeting to testify about recycling. Would you like to meet with them first?" Students can arrange these premeetings too. Their natural energy often tends to rocket them directly to their final target when a more circuitous path might be more effective in the end. There are times when your most effective move as mentor might be to set up a "time-out" space with lots of support (references, chart boards, refreshments) and encourage rethinking.

CIVIC ENGAGEMENT

When the time comes for students to influence their own local governmental officials directly, mentoring is especially important. In the *Young Voices for the Planet* films, both *Kids vs Global Warming* and

Whatever the project, student activism often attracts the press. Even if you think your students aren't making news, you should be prepared for contact from journalists. Here are a few tips:

- Minors should *never* be interviewed without written consent of their parents or guardians.

- While you can't—and shouldn't—rehearse students for interviews, it's a good idea to let them role-play themselves. "You may understand what you mean to say, but is there any chance it could be misunderstood?"

- Ask students to make short lists of solid facts to use in any conversation with a decision maker or a journalist.

- Teach students to "attract with honey." For example, ad hominem attacks ("The mayor is an idiot") are not nearly as effective as factual arguments.

- Take your own photos for distribution to news media (or ask a parent or another staff member to do it).

Team Marine show kids taking direct action to get things done in their own communities by communicating with their governmental officials.

Many educators hesitate to encourage students to get involved with their local governments because they fear being perceived as being overly political. That doesn't have to be the case. Consider these guidelines:

- Define the issue. Don't allow students' enthusiasm to be used by others who have different agendas.

- Don't let personalities become the focus. Avoid the "bad guy/good guy" paradigm.

- Help students study their own local governmental structure so they address their issues to the right agencies and right people, from the bottom up. (No point in protesting to the county board if the drain commissioner is willing to help solve the problem, or to the school board if the principal can make the change.)

- Prepare the facts in advance, and recheck them. Have note cards or PowerPoint presentations ready to make each meeting efficient. Quote respected scientists and have the data available.

- Clearly inform parents and other adults about what's planned. If transportation is an issue, define who is responsible.

- Be clear about what you want as an outcome. Have a reasonable, achievable goal for the meeting and the project. Think through the consequences (intended and unintended) of that goal.

- If the goal will affect others, get them involved. (For example, a project to ban plastic store bags would affect merchants. Ask a merchant to speak as well.)

- When students do attend public meetings, they should follow these guidelines:
  - Dress nicely.
  - Review the appropriate rules of conduct.
  - Review the agenda up front so they know how long they'll be waiting and when their turn to speak might occur.
  - Bring as many supporters as possible, but avoid "crowd behavior" like boos or cheers.
  - Decide in advance who will speak and how long.
  - Avoid direct arguments with those who don't agree.

- Teach students how to avoid being "derailed." Teach them how to stay on track and answer questions with the information they came to present.

FUNDRAISING

There's no such thing as a free lunch—and very rarely does a project come free. From buses and bumper stickers to seeds and trees, the raw materials of progress often require cash. As mentors for young activists, it's important for adults to help them select appropriate, effective, and safe ways to raise the funds they need.

First and foremost, it's important to make sure that the fundraising a group does is compatible with its goals. Dentists shouldn't give out candy bars, and environmentalists shouldn't sell plastic wristbands or water in plastic bottles! LED lightbulbs, power strips, cloth shopping bags, or seeds might make great fundraising projects and send the message, too.

Many groups rely on donations. Again, it's important to use good judgment. More than one group has found itself embarrassed when it was discovered that its funding came from a special interest group or an industry that didn't represent the group's cause well. An oil company or a corporation that generates toxic waste may get a lot of good press from a donation to a student ecology club, but the club won't—even if the donor asks nothing of the club in return. Many community organizations, from foundations to civic clubs, might be happy to support your group's project as long as it avoids direct politics.

When students are doing fundraising as part of a school-sponsored club or activity, the mentor or adult coordinator assumes a certain level of responsibility and unavoidable liability. Commonsense rules include the following:

- Inform parents early and thoroughly.
- Never sell anything that could be potentially dangerous.
- Never sell anything made of plastic or Styrofoam that will be used once and then thrown away.
- When selling products, try to get them made of materials that are biodegradable.
- Define the students' financial responsibility for the products very clearly.
- Students should not sell door-to-door except to homes of families they know.
- If students sell near a business, get permission from the business owner or manager.
- Instruct students that they should never give out personal information.
- Instruct students that they should never meet strangers off-site or get into a stranger's car.
- Set reasonable goals; don't expect great financial gains.
- Think of ways to accomplish more with less.
- Don't distribute paper (flyers) or other products that pollute!

Some projects have the potential to fund themselves, literally. Can a poster or idea be registered? Can an *appropriate* ad fund your website? Can a small membership fee be part of the adult community's involvement?

CAUTIONARY TALES

While the second part of this book is meant to be both energizing and encouraging, we want to emphasize also that it is vitally important that any mentor use common sense and conduct due diligence in planning and encouraging student effort. The following list of cautions is certainly not comprehensive, but it does indicate the sorts of commonsense steps that any caring adult would take to make positive outcomes and safe experiences far more likely:

- Check out all the players. Every volunteer for a student project (mentor, peer helper, volunteer) should be checked out. The formality of the vetting may vary from situation to situation, but some kind of check should always be part of the system.

- Conduct needed training. Never assume that adult volunteers such as chaperones know how to do their duties. Brainstorming and sharing a set of guidelines are always the minimal steps to take. If the project involves travel, more formal steps are probably needed.

- Put all guidelines and permissions, as well as the commitments of the participants, in writing. This helps everyone. There is never an excuse to say, "I didn't know" or "I thought that was someone else's responsibility."

- Obtain access permissions. Whenever a project is going to occur on private property, specific permissions are necessary. Such permissions may also be necessary on some public properties.

- Investigate the need for insurance. When in doubt, ask. It's not beyond the imagination that someone could trip and fall.

- Consider possible publications. Will there be photos? If so, where will they be used? Obtaining permissions is always appropriate, and it is especially vital if any of the photos, films, or interviews will be published.

- Decide how funds will be handled. Will money be collected and deposited in a bank account? If so, whose account? Will there be enough funds that the group must obtain a tax status?

- Decide how any sales will be handled. Is it safe for students to sell door-to-door? Must students travel in supervised groups?

- Consider the use of social media. In today's world, almost every situation is a potential source for social media. Your project is likely to eventually have Web exposure, and many communications about it will be disseminated by other electronic means. Don't wait until it happens to think about what could go wrong. Establish guidelines in advance:
  - Who is responsible for the main social media site?
  - Who proofs and approves that site?
  - Who is allowed to use the group's name and/or logo to make public statements or respond to questions from the press?

- What are the guidelines for publication?
- When students take their own photos, create podcasts, or tweet about the project, how do they avoid "speaking for the group" or publishing photos without permission?

- Plan for maintaining records and data. Everyone eventually moves on to new projects. Group records are vital. Make sure you establish a routine, a storage site, and a backup for the records of everything you've done.

AND WITH ALL THAT, DON'T TURN DOWN THE POWER!

The list of cautions could be much longer, but the message is clear. With forethought and planning, you can direct everyone's energy in a positive way without undue stress or strain. With cooperation and common goals, every project can provide good results. And with the proper encouragement, millions of *Young Voices for the Planet* can be heard around the world.

So don't hesitate. Don't discourage. Don't delay. Turn up the volume of a young voice near you!

Remember that the *Young Voices for the Planet* films are available on DVD through the Young Voices for the Planet website (Young VoicesforthePlanet.com). Teachers, you can download the films from the website for free or purchase the DVD. For institutional screenings, the producer requests that you purchase the DVD (http://www .youngvoicesonclimatechange.com/store.php). Thank you!

Last but not least, we want to keep in touch. Please post your youth carbon reduction success stories on our Young Voices on Climate Change Facebook page. And be sure to visit the interactive map at the Young Voices for the Planet website to put your school on the climate change action map!

Appendix I

Reproducible Student Sheets

Activity sheets for your students are provided in this section. You can photocopy the sheets from here or download them from http://www.youngvoicesonclimatechange.com.

Name:_____   Date:_____

Student Sheet for Activity 1.2   Empowering Young Voices for the Planet

Here's a challenge. Each of the scientists named below is involved in climate change research. But all the scientists have very different backgrounds and each uses different methods.

You can find information on some of the scientists in the book *How We Know What We Know About Our Changing Climate: Scientists and Kids Explore Global Warming*. Or you can use the Internet to find information on each of them.

(Be careful. There might be other people with similar names. You are looking for researchers who study the climate of the Earth.)

For each scientist, find out one problem that he or she researched or is researching. Find one or more of the practices of science that the scientist has used. Then imagine you could meet this scientist. Carefully craft one question you'd ask that scientist in person about his or her research.

Practices of Science

1. Asking questions and defining problems

2. Developing and using models

3. Planning and carrying out investigations

4. Analyzing data

5. Using mathematics

6. Creating explanations and solutions

7. Using evidence to argue a position

8. Obtaining, evaluating, and communicating information

TABLE 1.2.1 Climate Scientists and Their Research

SCIENTIST	PROBLEM	SCIENCE PRACTICES	QUESTION YOU WOULD ASK
Richard Norris			
Terry Root			
Steve Schneider			
Lisa Shaffer			
James Hansen			

Now imagine one of these scientists writes you and asks you, "What will you do to help solve the problem you have asked me about?" Use the Internet or your own imagination to write a response to the scientist's challenge.

_____

_____

_____

_____

_____

_____

_____

• • •

RISING SEA LEVELS, SINKING HOPES

Name:_____

Date:_____

Student Sheet for Activity 1.3

Empowering Young Voices for the Planet

With global warming, sea level will rise. That's because water expands when it warms up and because glaciers and ice masses melt more as temperature increases. Try this exercise to show how global warming and sea-level rise could affect New York City.

FIGURE 1.3.1

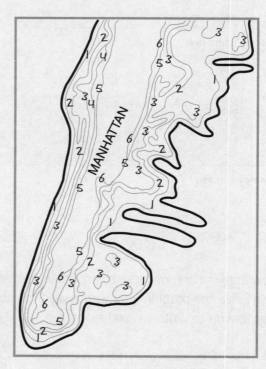

I. Use a topographic map to show sea-level rise.

Look at the topographic map of Manhattan in New York City at right. A topographic map shows how the land surface varies. It does this with contour lines. Each of the contour lines connects points of the same elevation. The number on the contour line tells you what that elevation is, in meters.

1. What areas of Manhattan, a section of New York City, will be underwater if sea level rises by each amount? (a) 1 m; (b) 2 m; (b) 3 m; (c) 4 m; (d) 5 m; (e) 6 m.

Use colored pencils to outline the contour lines for each of these changes to sea level.

2. Next, color in the flooded areas. Use a different color for each level of sea-level rise.

II. The map below shows the areas of the Florida coast that would be underwater if sea level were to rise 6 meters. That's a very large rise in sea level, but it is possible in extreme global warming scenarios.

Identify the Florida cities that would be underwater if the sea level rose 6 meters. Write the names of the cities next to the map. Use a reference to name more cities not shown on this map.

Florida cities flooded with a 6-meter rise in sea level:

FIGURE 1.3.2

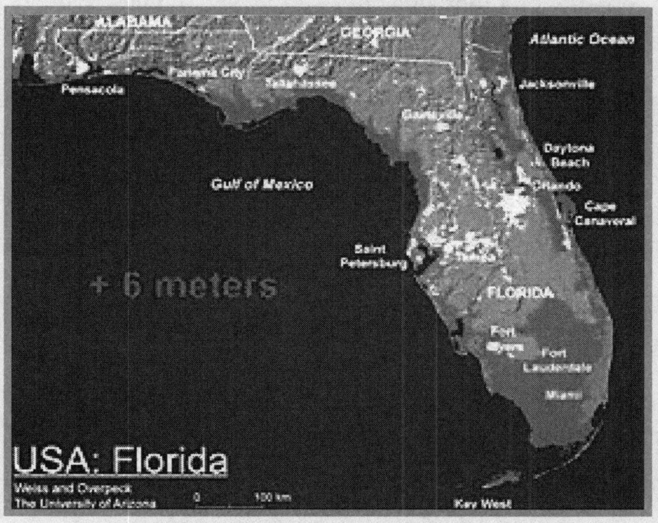

SOURCE: Weiss and Overpeck, University of Arizona.

_____

_____

_____

_____

_____

_____

_____

● ● ●

WHAT HAPPENS TO WHAT'S IN THE RECYCLING BIN?

Name:_____   Date:_____

Student Sheet for Activity 3.3   Empowering Young Voices for the Planet

There are at least seven kinds of plastics in a typical home. Not all are easily recycled with our current technology. In order to begin recycling, processors must separate different kinds of plastics. They normally do this by shredding them and then separating them by density. Your teacher has given you some shreds of common plastics and the five solutions shown in Table 3.3.1.

TABLE 3.3.1 Solutions for Testing the Density of Plastics

SOLUTION	AMOUNT ALCOHOL	AMOUNT WATER	AMOUNT SUGAR	MASS	DENSITY
1	100 mL	40 mL			.91 g/mL
2	80 mL	40 mL			.93 g/mL
3		150 mL			1.0 g/mL
4	150 mL				0.78 g/mL
5		150 mL	75 g		1.14 g/mL

The densities of common plastics are as follows:

PETE (polyethylene terephthalate)   1.38 g/mL

HDPE (high-density polyethylene)   0.95 g/mL

LDPE (low-density polyethylene)   0.94 g/mL

PP (polypropylene)   0.91 g/mL

PS (polystyrene)   1.06 g/mL

Lexan (polycarbonate)   1.2 g/mL

PVC (polyvinyl chloride)   1.16–1.38 g/mL

Now, drop your shreds into the various solutions. CAUTION: Be sure to wear eye protection! Observe and record whether they sink or float, using Table 3.3.2. Based on your observations, estimate the density of each sample. What kind of plastic could each sample be? (*Hint*: If a material floats, its density is less than the density of the surrounding fluid. If it sinks, the material is denser than the surrounding fluid.)

TABLE 3.3.2 Identifying Plastics by Density

PLASTIC SAMPLE	FLOATS OR SINKS IN SOLUTION?	DENSITY RANGE	TYPE OF PLASTIC
1			
2			
3			
4			
5			

● ● ●

▪ ▪ ▪ ▪ ▪ ▪ ▪ ▪ ▪ ▪ ▪ ▪ ▪ ▪ ▪ ▪ ▪ ▪ ▪

Name:_____

Date:_____

Student Sheet for Activity 3.4

Empowering Young Voices for the Planet

What could you do today that might affect your great-grandchildren? The answer is easy! Make a little less trash. Begin with a class project:

1. Dig a hole in the soil just outside your classroom.

2. Into that hole put at least six items that represent the typical things you might throw "away,"* such as:

- A plastic water bottle
- A plastic grocery bag
- A paper cup or plate
- A fruit or vegetable
- A preserved food snack (such as Twinkies)
- Cotton cloth (such as a rag or T-shirt)
- A piece of wood

3. Cover the items with dirt. Observe them once a week or when your teacher tells you to.

Once you have made your trash pit, answer these questions:

1. How long will it take each item to decompose? Check your predictions at the end of the year.

_____

_____

2. How is the observation pit you built like a landfill? How is it different?

_____

_____

Work the numbers:

There are *308,745,538* people living in the United States (2010 census). How much trash do the American people "throw away"?* Calculate:

3. If each person used one plastic water bottle a day, how many bottles would be used in the United States in a year?_____

4. Find the mass of a single empty plastic water bottle. How many tons of plastic would one-a-day use by every person in the United States produce in a year?_____

5. Use the Internet to determine how long a plastic water bottle lasts. _____

6. If you could influence 30 people to give up using plastic water bottles for a year, how much less plastic would your great-grandchildren have to clean up? _____

*There is no "away."

• • •

Name:_____   Date:_____

Student Sheet for Activity 4.2   Empowering Young Voices for the Planet

The data in the table below are adapted from research on the Kuparuk River in the Arctic, near the place where Anya did her research. The Kuparuk River is a fairly small, clear, and winding river. Scientists who work there want to know how nutrients brought into the river affect the river's health, including the amount of algae growing in it. They study nutrients such as nitrogen (N) and phosphorus (P) by adding them to the river system and watching the effects.

Directions

1. Make a line graph of the chlorophyll concentrations in the portions of the river that the scientists did not add nutrients to from 1983 to 1998. This is your reference graph.

2. With a different colored pencil, graph the chlorophyll in the fertilized portion of the river.

TABLE 4.2.1 Chlorophyll Comparison in the Kuparuk River

YEAR	AVERAGE WATER TEMP (°C)	AVERAGE RIVER FLOW (M³/CM)	REFERENCE CHLOROPHYLL (μG/CM²)	FERTILIZED CHLOROPHYLL (μG/CM²)
1983		1.2	0.04	2.73
1984		4.0	0.20	0.90
1985	9.0	2.1	0.94	2.23
1986	9.1	2.6	0.35	1.40
1987		3.5	0.16	0.26
1988	8.8	1.3	0.62	8.93
1989	10.5	2.8	0.37	3.31
1990	12.9	0.4	0.49	0.87
1991	9.6	1.7	0.27	1.73
1992	9.8	2.2	0.54	0.64
1993	10.1	2.9	0.13	0.26
1994	10.3	2.7	0.05	0.06
1995	8.8	4.2	0.19	0.36
1996	8.2	2.2	0.16	0.33
1997	9.8	2.8	0.19	0.34
1998	10.9		0.15	0.59

Now, answer the following questions.

Questions

1. What factors can affect the flow of an Arctic river?

_____

_____

_____

2. Why do we measure chlorophyll?

_____

_____

_____

3. When scientists added nutrients to the river, how did chlorophyll change?

_____

_____

_____

4. What effects would these changes have on other parts of the food chain?

_____

_____

_____

5. In recent years less snow in the Andes has reduced the water flow to rain-forest rivers. River flow slows and some areas become shallow lakes in the dry season. What do data from the Arctic tell us about the potential changes in the Amazon?

_____

_____

_____

• • •

Name:_____   Date:_____

Student Sheet for Activity 4.3   Empowering Young Voices for the Planet

FIGURE 4.3.1

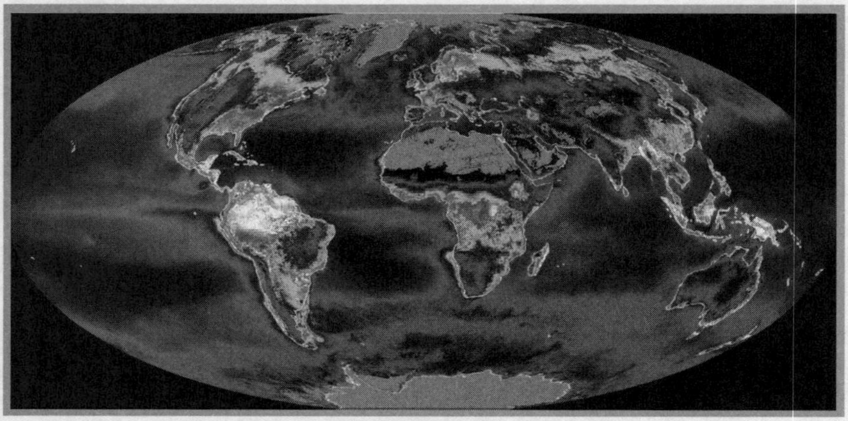

1. Look at this map of the world closely. It shows the *productivity* of ocean water. (That's the rate of photosynthesis, or how much carbon dioxide is bonded or *fixed* to make sugars.) Choose one area of the ocean that has a higher productivity than other areas at the same latitude.

2. Ask yourself: Why is the area you picked so productive? Think of what is needed for photosynthesis and what variables might affect that process. List some variables here.

_____

_____

3. Form a hypothesis about the source of the nutrients by filling in the blanks in the following:
   If _____ are greater than in other ecosystems, then _____ will be higher.

4. Use Internet sources to test your hypothesis. For example, you could check out sea surface temperatures or rainfall at http://earthobservatory.nasa.gov/GlobalMaps, or you could identify the high-population areas (cities) near the shores of an area.

5. Now write a sentence stating your conclusions about productivity and its possible source. Circle the right boldface words and then finish the sentence below.

Evidence supports/does not support the hypothesis that _____

_____

_____

• • •

Name:_____   Date:_____

Student Sheet for Activity 5.1   Empowering Young Voices for the Planet

Imagine you could fly like a bird and observe like a biologist. What might you see? What could you learn? Let's start on the island of Hispaniola (the first place Christopher Columbus saw in the New World).

FIGURE 5.1.1

SOURCE: NASA/Goddard Space Flight Center. (2014). *SVS Animation 2640—Haitian Deforestation.* Retrieved from http://commons.wikimedia.org/wiki/File:Haiti_deforestation.jpg.

1. The image shows the border between Haiti and the Dominican Republic. What difference can you observe? _____

_____

_____

2. With a pencil, draw a grid over the photo. Make each square 1 cm × 1cm. Count the total number of squares in each sector, and then count the number that are dark (green if viewed online). (Estimate fractions.) Then divide the forested area by the total area and multiply by 100. What is the percentage of Haiti that is forested? _____ What percentage of the Dominican Republic is forested? _____

_____

3. Brainstorm three effects that the difference in forestation might cause for each country:

_____

_____

4. Finally, go to the Earthshots website at http://earthshots.usgs.gov/earthshots/node/47#ad-image-0 and look at the changes in Orlando, Florida, from 1973 to 2011. Enlarge the photos and print them so you can make a grid that shows the development of Disney World. (Human development is white.)

   Use the same mathematical technique that you used in Step 2 to determine how much open space was lost by development. Be sure to draw your grid over the same area in each photo. How much open space was lost in the area of Orlando you have selected between 1973 and 2011? _____

FIGURE 5.1.2A Orlando, Florida, USA (1973)

FIGURE 5.1.2B Orlando, Florida, USA (2011)

SOURCE: U.S. Geological Survey. (2014). *Earthshots: Satellite Images of Environmental Change.* Retrieved from http://earthshots.usgs.gov/earthshots/node/47#ad-image-0.

_____

_____

_____

_____

_____

PLANT FOR THE PLANET—
AND FOR OUR FUTURE

Name:_____   Date:_____

Student Sheet for Activity 5.2   Empowering Young Voices for the Planet

What do plants add to the air that animals need to live? Here is a thought experiment: Imagine you were going to create a closed habitat in a soda bottle. Suppose you put plants (grass and clover) in the bottle, along with some of the following animals: worms, insects (like ants), tiny toads, or mice. Which combination of animals and plants will stay healthy even though the bottle is sealed? Use the data shown in Table 5.2.1 and Figure 5.2.2 to answer this question.

FIGURE 5.2.1 Soda Bottle: Fill it with the right combination of organisms to make an ecosystem.

TABLE 5.2.1   Masses of Organisms

ORGANISM	TOTAL MASS
Clover	2g per cm²
Worm	2g
Ants (6)	2g
Small toad	4g
Small mouse	6g

FIGURE 5.2.2 Average Oxygen Each Organism Uses or Provides per Minute

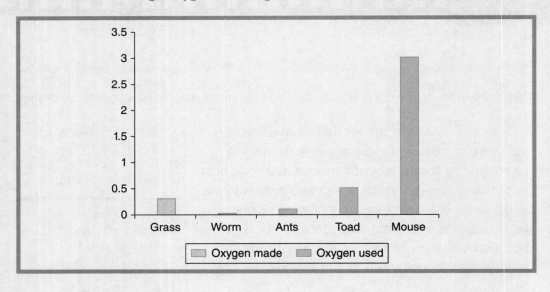

Think! Answer these questions:

1. Which organisms produce oxygen? Which need oxygen?

_____

2. Which organisms release carbon dioxide? Which use up carbon dioxide?

_____

3. What organisms can't we see in the jar? What do they need?

_____

4. Which organisms eat plants?

_____

5. Which animals would eat the other animals?

_____

6. What will happen in the jar in a day? In a week?

_____

7. How is a closed jar like our planet Earth?

_____

• • •

WHAT A DIFFERENCE A TREE MAKES!

Name:_____   Date:_____

Student Sheet for Activity 6.3   Empowering Young Voices for the Planet

Imagine you are a door-to-door sales-person. You are selling tree seedlings. In each row of the first column of the chart below, there is a fact about trees. In the second column, write a "sales pitch" to convince potential buyers to buy seedlings using the fact. In the third column, think of the response a potential buyer might make or a question he or she might ask.

FACT	SALES PITCH	RESPONSE
A healthy tree stores 13 pounds (5.9 kg) of carbon dioxide each year.		
A tree near a house can reduce air-conditioning costs by 30 percent.		
A tree absorbs 10 pounds (4.55 kg) of pollutants each year, including 3 pounds (1.36 kg) of soot that would otherwise land on windows and get in the house.		
A tree adds about 1 percent to the sales value of a home.		
A tree absorbs rainwater and prevents flooding of storm sewers during heavy storms. This reduces tax costs for water management about $10 per year.		
An average mature fruit tree can provide up to $100 of fresh local food per year for a family.		

Now that you have educated your potential customer, ask: "What would you like to pay for this tree?" What should the answer be? _____

• • •

WHO'S THE AUTHORITY?
A CREDIBILITY WEB QUEST

Name:_____   Date:_____

Student Sheet for Activity 7.1   Empowering Young Voices for the Planet

In this activity, you will dig a little deeper to check for bias in published information. You'll begin with a web search into the issue of *climate change.*

1. With a partner, identify three search terms that can produce a list of information-rich sources.

2. Go to a search engine recommended by your teacher and examine the hits.
   - Eliminate those that are commercial.
   - Eliminate "secondary" sources (opinion articles and blog sites).
   - Eliminate sites that are sponsored by companies.

3. Try another combination of three search terms. Use the same criteria as above to eliminate sites. Choose the list that produces the best choices to proceed.

4. From the hits that you've identified, do the following:
   - Choose five sources that support the idea of *anthropogenic* (human-caused) climate change.
   - Choose five sources that question the idea of *anthropogenic* climate change.

5. For each of those sources, identify the author. Answer the following questions for each author.

   A. Who wrote the paper or article?
      - Is she or he a scientist or a journalist?
      - Does the author have a reputation in the scientific world?
      - Has the author been employed by a commercial firm?

   B. If the author has a website, investigate who supports this person's work—her or his employer or institution. (See the example in Figure 7.1.1.)
      - Scroll to the bottom. Investigate the properties of the site.
      - Investigate the funding sources and other supporters of the site.

   C. Was the paper or article published in a well-respected scientific journal?
      - Was the article peer-reviewed* by other scientists in the field?
      - Do the article's references include commercial or political sources?
      - What was the funding source for the publication and the writer?

FIGURE 7.1.1

Image used with permission.

6. Finally, make a chart of your results with six columns, as below:

WEBSITE	AUTHOR	VIEWPOINT	REVIEWED?	SPONSORED?	IS THIS AN INDEPENDENT, SCIENTIFIC REPORT?

*A "peer-reviewed" article has been evaluated by other, unbiased scientists. Usually scholarly *journals* publish peer-reviewed articles.

• • •

Activity 8.1

A LONG TRIP FOR A LITTLE BIRD

Name:_____   Date:_____

Student Sheet for Activity 8.1   Empowering Young Voices for the Planet

Each spring the lengthening days send a message to a little bird—the Kirtland's warbler—on the islands of the Caribbean: "Fly north. Find exactly the right spot to make a nest and nurture a new generation." That place is a few hundred acres in northern Michigan near the city of Grayling, where the jack pine trees are just the right height and the sandy soil is exactly what the birds prefer. The birds' sun calendar brings them to those specific trees just in time to find hatching caterpillars, food for their own hatchlings.

Two threats caused the Kirtland population to dwindle almost to extinction: humans cut down many of the trees and changed the habitat, and birds of another species—cowbirds—often snuck their own eggs into the warblers' nests. Since cowbird eggs hatch more quickly than warbler eggs, the newly hatched cowbirds got most of the tasty caterpillars and the new warbler babies starved. (The story of the effect of cowbirds on another migratory bird species, the wood thrush, can be found in Lynne Cherry's book *Flute's Journey: The Life of a Wood Thrush*.)

FIGURE 8.1.1 Migratory Route of the Kirtland's Warbler

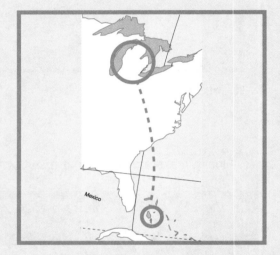

A massive effort to save the Kirtland's warbler had a lot of success. People realized that the jack pine forests had to be protected. The population began to grow again.

But in recent years, something changed. The average temperature of the northern forests is increasing. Think about how this might affect the life cycles of birds and insects.

106   EMPOWERING YOUNG VOICES FOR THE PLANET

1. Many birds migrate hundreds or thousands of miles each year. What is the advantage of migration?

_____

_____

_____

_____

2. Birds are warm-blooded (homeothermic), and caterpillars are cold-blooded (ectothermic). How would warming forests affect the hatching of the caterpillars?

_____

_____

_____

_____

3. How would a change in the hatching time of caterpillars affect the competition between little cowbirds and little warblers?

_____

_____

_____

_____

4. What other changes might occur in a northern forest if the average temperature continued to rise?

_____

_____

_____

_____

TAKE A WALK!

Name:_____

Date:_____

Student Sheet for Activity 9.3

Begin with a walking tour. Go to your local grocery store. You don't need to buy anything, but you'll need to read some *really small* labels, so you might want to bring along a hand lens.

Here's your shopping list. On each product, you'll find a small label showing the place where the food was produced. (It may say "Country of Origin"

Empowering Young Voices for the Planet

if the product was produced outside the United States. It may list several countries if the local distributor gets the product from several places.)

Then use a map or an Internet search engine to calculate how many miles the product traveled to reach your local store. One site you can use is http://www.geobytes.com/citydistancetool.htm.

PRODUCT	PLACE OF ORIGIN	MILES TRANSPORTED
Tomatoes		
Oranges		
Hamburger meat		
Celery		
Nuts (walnuts)		

FIGURE 9.3 MAP OF THE WORLD

SOURCE: http://commons.wikimedia.org/wiki/File:CIA_WorldFactBook-Political_world.pdf.

Name:_____   Date:_____

Student Sheet for Activity 9.4   Empowering Young Voices for the Planet

Each area of the country has its own special crops and its own growing seasons. But with greenhouses, good food storage, and cooperation, almost any region can harvest fresh food all year long. Of course, that takes planning.

1. Think about what sorts of edible plants you can you grow in your region. Consider:

   • *Space:* It's not practical to grow pumpkins in your classroom window. What could you grow? Investigate lettuce, radishes, sprouts, tomatoes, beans, peas, and cabbages. Perhaps you have more space than just your windowsill. Make a diagram of all of your potential growing spaces.

   • *Light:* Most edible plants need lots of light. What side of your building has the best light? How much space do you have in a location that receives lots of light throughout the day? (The farther north you are, the more this matters.)

   • *Temperature:* Will you grow inside or outside? If you have a greenhouse, does it have temperature control?

   • *Time:* How many people will be cooperating to help with your crops? Will you have help on the weekends?

2. Then investigate your community. What foods are available fresh during the year? The chart below shows harvest times. It can help you get started.

	POTATOES (OR RICE)	CORN	BEANS
Maryland	September	July	November
New Jersey	September	October	October
California	(Rice in May)	October	September
North Carolina	June	September	November
Missouri	June	August	October
New York	September	October	September
Florida	February	September	November

You can find more information at the following Web address: http://www.nass. usda.gov/Publications/Usual_Planting_ and_Harvesting_Dates/uph97.pdf. But don't stop with these crops. Many crops are very early or late—like asparagus in May or late carrots in November.

3. Now make a plan: Think about what would be available from your greenhouse or school or community garden twelve months of the year. Write it in a planning calendar such as the one below.

FRESH FOODS FROM LOCAL SOURCES

Jan	Feb	Mar	Apr	May	Jun	Jul	Aug	Sep	Oct	Nov	Dec

• • •

Appendix II

Teacher Support Material: Answers to Student Questions and List of Selected Standards

ANSWERS TO STUDENT QUESTIONS

Note to teachers and mentors: many of the calculations and activities in the text are similar to what scientists sometimes call "Fermi questions." They are modeled after the estimation challenges popularized by physicist Enrico Fermi. Estimations are fine in many of these activities; it's the basic idea that counts!

Intro Activity: Trains, Planes, and Automobiles

Gallons of gas for the trip from Washington, D.C., to Los Angeles:

Car: (2,700 miles) × (1 gal./21 miles) = 129 gal.

Plane: (2,700 miles) × (1 gal./23 miles) = 117 gal.

Train: (2,700 miles) × (1 gal./45 miles) = 60 gal.

Then:

Carbon dioxide consumed by plane versus car:

$117 - 60 = 57$ gal. × (20 lb. CO_2/gal.) = 1,140 lb. CO_2

Carbon dioxide consumed by train versus car:

$129 - 60 = 69$ gal. × (20 lb. CO_2/gal.) = 1,380 lb. CO_2

SCIENTIST	PROBLEM	PRACTICES OF SCIENCE[a]	QUESTION YOU WOULD ASK
Richard Norris http://cmbc.ucsd.edu/ People/Faculty_and_ Researchers/norris	Diversity of life (observation and population studies)	1, 2, 3, 4, 5, 6, 8	Will vary
Terry Root http://terryroot .stanford.edu	Climate change (studies bird populations)	1, 2, 3, 4, 5, 6, 7, 8	Will vary
Steve Schneider http://stephenschneider .stanford.edu	Climate change (editor and publisher)	1, 2, 3, 4, 7, 8	Will vary
Lisa Shaffer http://scrippsnews .ucsd.edu/Releases/? releaseID=130	Climate change (helps build bridges between scientists and government)	2, 4, 6, 7, 8	Will vary
James Hansen http://www.columbia .edu/~jeh1	Climate scientist (formerly of NASA, now runs independent agency)	1, 2, 3, 4, 5, 6, 7, 8	Will vary

a. The numbers in this column correspond to those in the list of practices of science that appears above Table 1.2.1 on the Activity 1.2 student sheet.

iMatter

SOURCE: Created by Alec Loorz for Kids vs Global Warming and iMatter.

1. Students will color-code the topographic map. Maps should look similar to the map shown here.

2. Cities located on the red areas of the Florida map include Jacksonville, Cape Canaveral, St. Petersburg, Daytona Beach, Miami, Fort Lauderdale, Key West, Tallahassee, Panama City, and Pensacola. If your students use a more detailed map, they can add other cities that are color-coded red.

FIGURE 1.3.1a

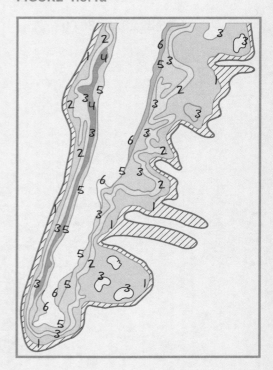

SOURCE: Created by Alec Loorz for Kids vs Global Warming and iMatter.

1. $46.85

2. $5,294,373,180.00

3. 8

• • •

iReduce

SOURCE: Created by Alec Loorz for Kids vs Global Warming and iMatter.

Here are some sample answers students might obtain.

PLASTIC SAMPLE	FLOATS OR SINKS IN SOLUTION?	DENSITY RANGE	TYPE OF PLASTIC
1	Sinks in all solutions	Density greater than 1.14 g/mL	PETE, Lexan, or PVC
2	Sinks in all solutions except alcohol	Density greater than 0.78 but less than 1.14 g/mL	HDPE, LDPE, PP, or PS
3	Floats in solutions 3 and 5; sinks in 1, 2, and 4	Density less than 1.0 g/mL but greater than 0.91 g/mL	LDPE or HDPE
4	Floats in solution 5; sinks in all others	Density less than 1.14 g/mL but greater than 1.0 g/mL	PS
5	Sinks in all solutions	Density greater than 1.14 g/mL	PETE, Lexan, or PVC

iRecycle

SOURCE: Created by Alec Loorz for Kids vs Global Warming and iMatter.

1. Answers will vary.

2. There are many differences, but students should note that the trash in the pit is covered and compressed by surrounding soil, which is rich in decomposing organisms.

3. 365 bottles per person × 308,745,538 people = 112,692,121,370 bottles.

4. Each bottle has a mass of about 13 grams. 365 bottles × 13 g = 4,745 g, almost 5 kg for one person; 4,745 g per person × 308,745,538 people = 1,464,997,577,810 g, or almost 1.5 trillion grams, which equals 15 billion grams.

5. In fact, no one knows! But at least 200 years.

6. 5 kg × 30 people = 150 kg.

• • •

iQuit

SOURCE: Created by Alec Loorz for Kids vs Global Warming and iMatter.

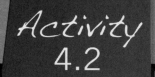
See the sample graph below: Series 1 is without fertilizer, and Series 2 is with fertilizer. Students should notice a very large algal bloom in the year 1988 and develop good questions about why that might happen.

GRAPH 4.2

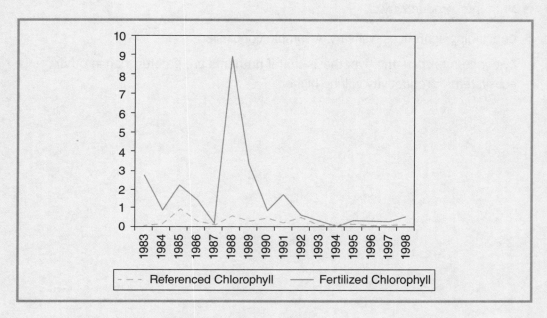

1. Rainfall, temperature, and winter snow melt can affect the flow of a river.

2. Chlorophyll is the chemical that makes photosynthesis happen. It's found in algae and plants, so it's a measure of how the plants grow.

3. Nutrients made the algae and plants bloom.

4. While there could be more photosynthesis at first, those algae will die and eventually use up the oxygen in the water.

5. When there is less water, there will be more oxygenation. Increased oxygen will eventually change the food web.

iMelt

SOURCE: Created by Alec Loorz for Kids vs Global Warming and iMatter.

2. Students should find a latitude (a line that can be drawn *across* the globe) that has different levels of productivity. (Student answers will vary.) Since the sunlight will be about the same and there's plenty of water and carbon dioxide, the differences must come from nutrients.

3. Nutrients, productivity.

5. Concluding sentences will vary. A sample conclusion:

Evidence **supports** the hypothesis that if nutrients are greater than in other ecosystems, productivity will be higher.

. . .

iWarm

SOURCE: Created by Alec Loorz for Kids vs Global Warming and iMatter.

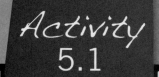

1. Students should be able to clearly observe the ridge that separates the Dominican Republic from Haiti.

2. While students are doing estimations, they should all be able to calculate that Haiti (in this area) is less than 10 percent forested, while the Dominican Republic is about 70 percent forested.

3. Accept all reasonable answers. Possible effects are erosion, landslides, and destruction of ecosystems.

4. In the images of Disney World, about 25 percent of the green space was lost in the process of development. Answers can vary if other areas of Orlando were selected.

• • •

iRestore

SOURCE: Created by Alec Loorz for Kids vs Global Warming and iMatter.

While students' models will vary, they should all reflect an understanding that the higher the order of consumer, the more oxygen consumed. So the grass in the graph produces only enough oxygen for a few ants.

1. All organisms (including plants) need oxygen, but only the plants produce oxygen.

2. All the animals produce carbon dioxide, and only the plants use carbon dioxide.

3. Many bacteria use oxygen and produce carbon dioxide. Some model ecosystem jars might also grow algae, which produce oxygen like plants. (There are photosynthetic bacteria, but they are unlikely to have much presence in a bottle biology jar.)

4. The ants and mouse may eat plants.

5. The toad eats other animals. The worm eats protozoans—both plantlike and animal-like single-celled organisms.

6. In the short term there might be extra oxygen in the jar, but later there would have to be many more plants.

7. Answers will vary, but students should understand that the Earth's capacity to maintain its atmosphere is limited.

• • •

SOURCE: Created by Alec Loorz for Kids vs Global Warming and iMatter.

Activity 6.3

WHAT A DIFFERENCE A TREE MAKES!

While students' answers will vary, check for facts. Does the proposed sales pitch reflect accurate science? Ideas about the selling price of a tree seedling will vary too. Ideally, the selling price for the seedling should reflect the tree's value to the biosphere as well as its standard market value, which might be between $5 and $20. Some students may argue that the seedlings should be sold on a sliding scale so that everyone who can take care of a tree can have one.

• • •

iPlant

SOURCE: Created by Alec Loorz for Kids vs Global Warming and iMatter.

This activity will be different for every group and student, but inevitably students will discover that the funders of websites are often surprising and hard to trace.

• • •

SOURCE: Created by Alec Loorz for Kids vs Global Warming and iMatter.

1. Organisms migrate to have better food supplies or fewer predators.

2. The caterpillars hatch earlier, but the birds and other warm-blooded animals have the same rate of maturity.

3. The cowbirds hatch earlier, and if the caterpillars hatch earlier, the cowbirds get more food earlier.

4. Less snowfall (less ice cover on lakes) makes drier springs; that can change the number and variety of certain plants, the germination of seeds, and the success of hatching of pond birds.

• • •

iBike

SOURCE: Created by Alec Loorz for Kids vs Global Warming and iMatter.

While their answers will vary, students will find that most tomatoes, oranges, celery, and nuts travel more than 1,000 miles to their local grocery. If they go to a national "big box" chain, they will find three or four possible countries of origin for the meat because suppliers vary.

• • •

iHang

SOURCE: Created by Alec Loorz for Kids vs Global Warming and iMatter.

While their answers will vary, students in almost all areas of the country should find that there are root crops that are healthy and very easily stored for months. For example, in Michigan students might include carrots and potatoes for all the winter months; in Florida mangoes last through July, and tomatoes can be grown almost all year.

• • •

iPower

SOURCE: Created by Alec Loorz for Kids vs Global Warming and iMatter.

SELECTED STANDARDS

Next Generation Science Standards

Practices of Science for K–12 Science Classrooms

1. Asking questions (for science) and defining problems (for engineering)
2. Developing and using models
3. Planning and carrying out investigations
4. Analyzing and interpreting data
5. Using mathematics and computational thinking
6. Constructing explanations (for science) and designing solutions (for engineering)
7. Engaging in argument from evidence
8. Obtaining, evaluating, and communicating information

Selected Next Generation Science Standards: Middle School

ESS2.D: Weather and Climate

- Weather and climate are influenced by interactions involving sunlight, the ocean, the atmosphere, ice, landforms, and living things. These interactions vary with latitude, altitude, and local and regional geography, all of which can affect oceanic and atmospheric flow patterns. (MS-ESS2-6)

- Because these patterns are so complex, weather can only be predicted probabilistically. (MS-ESS2-5)

- The ocean exerts a major influence on weather and climate by absorbing energy from the sun, releasing it over time, and globally redistributing it through ocean currents. (MS-ESS2-6)

ESS3.A: Natural Resources

- Humans depend on Earth's land, ocean, atmosphere, and biosphere for many different resources. Minerals, fresh water, and biosphere resources are limited, and many are not renewable or replaceable over human lifetimes. These resources are distributed unevenly around the planet as a result of past geologic processes. (MS-ESS3-1)

ESS3.B: Natural Hazards

- Mapping the history of natural hazards in a region, combined with an understanding of related geologic forces, can help forecast the locations and likelihoods of future events. (MS-ESS3-2)

ESS3.C: Human Impacts on Earth Systems

- Human activities have significantly altered the biosphere, sometimes damaging or destroying natural habitats and causing the extinction of other species. But changes to Earth's environments can have different impacts (negative and positive) for different living things. (MS-ESS3-3)

- Typically as human populations and per-capita consumption of natural resources increase, so do the negative impacts on Earth unless the activities and technologies involved are engineered otherwise. (MS-ESS3-3), (MS-ESS3-4)

ESS3.D: Global Climate Change

- Human activities, such as the release of greenhouse gases from burning fossil fuels, are major factors in the current rise in Earth's mean surface temperature (global warming). Reducing the level of climate change and reducing human vulnerability to whatever climate changes do occur depend on the understanding of climate science, engineering capabilities, and other kinds of knowledge, such as understanding of human behavior, and on applying that knowledge wisely in decisions and activities. (MS-ESS3-5)

Sample Common Core Standards: English Language Arts—Science and Technical Subjects

Integration of Knowledge and Ideas

CCSS.ELA-Literacy.RST.6-8.7

- Integrate quantitative or technical information expressed in words in a text with a version of that information expressed visually (e.g., in a flowchart, diagram, model, graph, or table).

CCSS.ELA-Literacy.RST.6-8.8

- Distinguish among facts, reasoned judgment based on research findings, and speculation in a text.

CCSS.ELA-Literacy.RST.6-8.9

- Compare and contrast the information gained from experiments, simulations, video, or multimedia sources with that gained from reading a text on the same topic.

Range of Reading and Level of Text Complexity

CCSS.ELA-Literacy.RST.6-8.10
- By the end of grade 8, read and comprehend science/technical texts in the grades 6–8 text complexity band independently and proficiently.

Sample Common Core Standards: Mathematics—Statistics and Probability Grade 6

Develop understanding of statistical variability.

CCSS.Math.Content.6.SP.A.1

- Recognize a statistical question as one that anticipates variability in the data related to the question and accounts for it in the answers.

CCSS.Math.Content.6.SP.A.2

- Understand that a set of data collected to answer a statistical question has a distribution which can be described by its center, spread, and overall shape.

Use random sampling to draw inferences about a population.

CCSS.Math.Content.7.SP.A.1

- Understand that statistics can be used to gain information about a population by examining a sample of the population; generalizations about a population from a sample are valid only if the sample is representative of that population. Understand that random sampling tends to produce representative samples and support valid inferences.

CCSS.Math.Content.7.SP.A.2

- Use data from a random sample to draw inferences about a population with an unknown characteristic of interest. Generate multiple samples (or simulated samples) of the same size to gauge the variation in estimates or predictions.

Draw informal comparative inferences about two populations.

CCSS.Math.Content.7.SP.B.3

- Informally assess the degree of visual overlap of two numerical data distributions with similar variabilities, measuring the difference between the centers by expressing it as a multiple of a measure of variability.

Appendix III

Resources for Further Exploration

WEBSITES

1. Young Voices for the Planet (Lynne Cherry's website): http://www.youngvoicesonclimatechange.com

2. iMatter (Alec Loorz's website): http://www.imatteryouth.org

3. Intergovernmental Panel on Climate Change: http://www.ipcc.ch

4. National Geographic, Light Bulb Savings Calculator: http://environment.nationalgeographic.com/environment/energy/great-energy-challenge/light-bulb-savings-calculator

5. Urban EcoLab (for many activities related to various topics): http://urbanecolabcurriculum.com

6. Teaching Issues and Experiments in Ecology (data sets for Arctic LTER): http://tiee.ecoed.net/vol/v3/issues/data_sets/arc/data.html

7. Institute of Scrap Recycling Industries (for activities related to recycling): http://www.isri.org

8. Long Term Ecological Research Network: http://www.lternet.edu

9. Polar Field Services (Max Holmes's LTER website): http://www.polarfield.com/blog/tag/nsf-arctic-research-program

10. Plant-for-the-Planet (Felix Finkbeiner's website): http://www.plant-for-the-planet.org

11. Earthshots: Satellite Images of Environmental Change, U.S. Geological Survey: http://earthshots.usgs.gov/earthshots

12. U.S. Department of Agriculture, "Usual Planting and Harvesting Dates for U.S. Field Crops": http://www.nass.usda.gov/Publications/Usual_Planting_and_Harvesting_Dates/uph97.pdf

13. Geobytes, City Distance Tool: http://www.geobytes.com/citydistance tool.htm

14. Earth Observatory, NASA (images): http://earthobservatory.nasa.gov/Images/?eocn=topnav&eoci=images

15. Green Ambassadors Institute: http://greenambassadors.org

16. Climate Change Resource Center, U.S. Forest Service: http://www.fs.fed.us/ccrc

17. Lynne Cherry author website: www.lynnecherry.com

18. Suzanne Lyons educational products websites featuring cooperative games and tools for connecting children and nature: www.childandnature.com and www.cooperativegames.com

19. The Team Marine project website: www.teammarine.org

20. The Local Lunch website: http://projectsprout.org/

21. Latest information and Olivia's projects and access to her YouTube channel: http://www.oliviabouler.net/artwork--book.html

22. Program information about Dreaming in Green: http://dreamingreen.org/

23. The CLEAN network: http://cleanet.org/clean/community/cln/index.html

BOOKS

1. Cherry, Lynne, and Gary Braasch. *How We Know What We Know About Our Changing Climate: Scientists and Kids Explore Global Warming.* Nevada City, CA: Dawn, 2010.

2. Burns, Lore Griffin, and Ellen Harasimowicz, Ellen. *Citizen Scientists: Be a Part of Scientific Discovery From Your Own Backyard.* New York: Henry Holt, 2012.

3. Simon, Seymour. *Global Warming.* New York: HarperCollins, 2012.

4. Trautmann, Nancy M., Jennifer Fee, Terry M. Tomasek, and NancyLee R. Bergey. *Citizen Science: 15 Lessons That Bring Biology to Life.* Arlington, VA: NSTA Press, 2013.

5. Bouler, Olivia. *Olivia's Birds: Saving the Gulf.* New York: Sterling, 2011.

Important Terms Related to Climate Change

activism: Intentional action to bring about social, economic, political, or environmental change.

adaptation to climate change: Adjustment or preparation of human systems to deal with changes in the natural environment produced by a changing climate.

alternative energy: Energy that comes from nontraditional sources, including solar, wind, and geothermal.

anthropogenic climate change: Alteration to the climate produced by human activities. This is opposed to variations in Earth's climate that have occurred over geologic time due to natural causes, such as variations in Earth's orbit, volcanic eruptions, and plate tectonic activity.

biofuels: Gaseous or liquid fuels derived from biomass, such as wood or ethanol.

biomass: (1) The amount of living matter residing in a given habitat, expressed in units of weight per area or volume of organisms per volume of habitat. (2) Energy obtained from organisms, including ethanol (from crops or from grasses, trees, and other plants that are being harvested anyway) and biodiesel (old cooking oil).

carbon cycle: The transfer of carbon atoms between the tissues of living organisms and Earth's crust, atmosphere, and waters. Carbon exists in the abiotic world mainly as carbon dioxide in the atmosphere and dissolved carbon dioxide in the oceans. During photosynthesis, producers move carbon to the biotic world. Carbon then passes up the food chain. Carbon is returned to the abiotic world as carbon dioxide, a product of cellular respiration. The burning of fossil fuels, which releases a huge amount of carbon previously trapped in the fuels, has become an important part of the carbon cycle over the past century.

carbon footprint: The total amount of greenhouse gases that are emitted into the atmosphere each year by any entity, such as a person, family, building, or company. An individual's carbon footprint includes greenhouse gas emissions from any fuel that the individual uses, such as riding in a car. It also includes greenhouse gases generated to produce the goods or services that the individual uses, such as emissions from power plants that make electricity, factories that make products, mines that extract raw materials, and landfills where trash is deposited.

carbon sequestration: The process by which trees and plants absorb carbon dioxide, release the oxygen, and store the carbon.

civic engagement: Acting upon a sense of responsibility to one's community. Also called *community engagement*.

climate: The long-term, average pattern of weather in a particular area. Climate is measured in terms of weather variables (including precipitation, temperature, wind, and humidity) over periods of thirty years or more.

climate change: Significant change in the measures of climate lasting for an extended period of time.

climate model: A quantitative representation of interactions of climate variables. Some models are relatively simple while others are very complex and comprehensive. Climate models use data that describe the atmosphere, land surface, oceans, and ice.

coal: A fossil fuel produced by plants that grew in ancient swamps and then were compacted over geologic time.

deforestation: Processes by which forested lands are converted to nonforest uses. Deforestation contributes to increasing carbon dioxide concentrations for two reasons: (1) the burning or decomposition of the wood releases carbon dioxide through chemical combustion; and (2) trees that once took carbon dioxide from the atmosphere for photosynthesis are no longer present to act as carbon sinks.

desertification: The reduction or loss of the biological productivity of rain-fed cropland, irrigated cropland, or range, pasture, forest, and woodlands resulting from land uses or processes arising from human activities and habitation patterns.

Earth system: The atmosphere, lithosphere, biosphere, cryosphere, and hydrosphere taken together as an interdependent whole. From the systems perspective, planetary feedbacks, emergent properties, and other systems properties are considered as well as the individual parts and processes within the system.

ecosystem: Living and nonliving elements that interact to produce a stable system through the cyclic exchange of materials.

enhanced greenhouse effect: An intensified greenhouse effect resulting from high concentrations of greenhouse gases exhausted into the atmosphere from human activities.

fossil fuels: Combustible organic material such as oil, coal, or natural gas derived from the remains of ancient life, exposed to heat and pressure in the Earth's crust over hundreds of millions of years. Since fossil fuels derive from once-living organisms, they are composed of biomolecules, the molecules of life. Biomolecules are carbon based and are rich sources of chemical energy, which they store in their chemical bonds. Combusting fossil fuels breaks the bonds within biomolecules, so that the carbon and energy within them are released.

fracking (hydraulic fracturing): A means of extracting natural gas from deep wells. Once a well is drilled, millions of gallons of water, sand, and chemicals are injected into it under high pressure. The pressure fractures underground rock (shale), which opens fissures in the rock so that natural gas can flow through it out of the well.

geothermal energy: Energy derived from heat in the interior of the Earth. Geothermal energy power plants use superheated water or steam from Earth's interior to turn turbines that generate electricity.

glacier: A mass of dense ice that forms when snow is subjected to pressure from overlying snow so that it is compacted and recrystallized. Glaciers are divided into two types: *alpine glaciers* (glaciers that occupy mountain valleys) and *continental glaciers* (glaciers that spread out as thick, relatively flat blocks of ice).

global average temperature: Earth's mean surface air temperature averaged over the entire planet.

greenhouse effect: The process by which certain gases in Earth's atmosphere—called *greenhouse gases*—trap heat, raising Earth's average temperature. That is, in Earth's lower atmosphere, greenhouse gases (including carbon dioxide, methane, and water vapor) allow the visible light emitted from the sun to pass through. Visible light, or "shortwave electromagnetic radiation," is absorbed when it reaches Earth's surface. Some of this energy is retained by the ground and warms the ground. However, much of the incoming shortwave radiation is converted to longer-wavelength infrared radiation at Earth's surface and is reemitted. Whereas the atmosphere, in particular greenhouse gases, lets visible light pass through, it does not readily transmit infrared radiation. Thus infrared radiation is detained in the lower atmosphere by greenhouse gases, raising the atmosphere's temperature, until the radiation eventually escapes into space. The greenhouse effect is a natural and necessary phenomenon. Without it, Earth's atmosphere would be a frigid −18°C. The present concern is the *enhanced greenhouse effect,* which results from human activity.

greenhouse gas: Any gas that absorbs long-wavelength (infrared) radiation in the atmosphere. Greenhouse gases include carbon dioxide and methane.

hydrologic cycle: The process by which water evaporates from Earth's surface or the ocean, moves vertically and horizontally through the atmosphere, condenses to form clouds, then precipitates to fall back to Earth's surface. The hydrologic cycle, also called the *water cycle,* is a major factor in determining climate through its influence on surface vegetation, clouds, snow and ice, and soil moisture.

hydropower: Energy (mostly electric) that is derived from the motion of falling water.

ice age: A geologic time period when Earth's average temperature is cold enough to support extensive glaciation. Earth is now in an ice age and has been ever since humans have inhabited the planet.

ice cap: A continental glacier with an area less than 50,000 square miles.

ice core: A cylindrical sample of ice removed from a glacier or an ice sheet that is studied to reveal information about climate patterns of the past. Scientists chemically analyze the air bubbles in ice cores to measure the percentages of carbon dioxide and other trace gases in the atmosphere at a given time.

ice sheet: A continental glacier with an area greater than 50,000 square miles (129,499 square kilometers).

Industrial Revolution: A period of unprecedented economic and technological expansion that began in the Western world in the early nineteenth century as machines were invented to do the work formerly done using hand tools and animals, and the factory system was invented. Fossil fuels were increasingly tapped as a source of energy to run the machines and factories of the Industrial Revolution, and they have been used extensively ever since.

infrared radiation: Electromagnetic radiation with a wavelength longer than the red color in the visible part of the spectrum, but shorter than microwave radiation. Infrared radiation can be perceived as heat when it is absorbed by the human body.

Intergovernmental Panel on Climate Change (IPCC): A global volunteer organization of more than 1,300 scientists from over sixty nations that reviews scientific research on climate change and summarizes it in reports for policy makers and the public.

landfill: A waste disposal site where waste is continually spread into thin layers, compacted, and covered with soil.

latitude: The position of a location north or south with respect to the equator. The equator is designated 0°; the North and South Poles are at latitude 90° north and south. Lines of latitude circle the globe and are parallel to one another.

methane: A greenhouse gas with the molecular formula CH_4. It is the second most prevalent greenhouse gas emitted in the United States by human activities. Pound for pound, methane has a global warming potential estimated at twenty-five times that of carbon dioxide (CO_2). Methane reaches the atmosphere through the anaerobic (without oxygen) decomposition of waste in landfills, through animal digestion and the decomposition of animal wastes, through the production and distribution of natural gas and petroleum, through coal production, and through incomplete fossil fuel combustion. Large deposits of methane are stored under the oceans and in the Arctic permafrost. The release of these stores of methane is a major concern with respect to climate change.

mountaintop removal: A form of coal mining that uses explosives to remove the tops of mountains to enable access to seams of coal.

natural gas: Underground deposits of gases that consist of between 50 percent and 90 percent methane, with smaller amounts of heavier hydrocarbon gases such as propane and butane.

oil: Liquid petroleum.

oil sands: Deposits of sticky, black oil (bitumen) that adheres to sediments deep underground; also called *tar sands*. The oil sands in Canada are a major source of fossil fuel for the United States.

parts per million (ppm): A unit used to quantify low concentrations of substances. There is scientific consensus that the safe upper limit for carbon dioxide in the atmosphere is 350 ppm. At a concentration of 350 ppm, 350 out of every 1 million molecules in the atmosphere would be carbon dioxide molecules. Recent reports indicate that Earth's atmosphere currently has a carbon dioxide concentration of approximately 400 ppm.

permafrost: Continually frozen ground where the temperature remains below 0°C for years.

petroleum: A mixture of fossil fuels and other gaseous and liquid hydrocarbons from compressed planktonic organisms.

photosynthesis: The process in plants and some other organisms in which light energy from the sun is converted to chemical energy stored in organic molecules.

producer: An organism that makes organic molecules using inorganic molecules and energy.

recycling: The process of collecting and reprocessing a resource so it can be used again.

reforestation: The planting of trees on land that once contained a forest but has been converted to some other use.

renewable energy: Energy that comes from renewable natural resources, such as sunlight, wind, geothermal heat, and tides.

resilience: The capacity to anticipate, prepare for, respond to, and recover from significant multi-hazard threats with minimum damage to social well-being, the economy, and the environment.

respiration: The process by which organisms use oxygen to convert organic materials to carbon dioxide and energy.

sea ice: Ice that is formed by the freezing of seawater. Sea ice takes up about 7 percent of the surface area of the world's oceans.

solar power: Energy generated from the sun's heat or light. Solar power can be used to produce electricity, to heat or cool air, to produce light, and to heat water.

solar radiation: Electromagnetic radiation emitted by the sun.

thermal expansion: An increase in the volume of a substance as its temperature increases. The warming of ocean water leads to an increase in its volume, which leads to a rise in sea level.

thermohaline circulation: Large-scale circulation of ocean water due to variations in the density of the water; also called the *global ocean conveyor* because thermohaline circulation distributes heat all over the world as it moves warm water from the equator generally toward the poles. Cold water is denser than warm water, and salty water is denser than less salty water. Thus both salinity and temperature can force ocean water to move. Currently, the circulation of seawater in the Atlantic is driven mainly by temperature differences. Water heated near the equator travels at the ocean surface into higher latitudes, where it loses heat to the atmosphere (which keeps the climate in North America relatively mild). The cooled Atlantic water sinks to the deep ocean near the North Pole and travels at great depths around the world, eventually resurfacing. The present concern is that the influx of freshwater from melting sea ice at high latitudes will disrupt thermohaline circulation, because the less dense water will no longer sink.

water vapor: Water in the gaseous state. Water vapor is a potent heat-trapping greenhouse gas, but it is not a subject of concern as carbon dioxide and methane are because it remains in equilibrium with the air.

watershed: Entire area of land that drains into a river.

weather: The state of the atmosphere at a given place and time with respect to the following variables: temperature, precipitation, cloudiness, humidity, air pressure, wind, and humidity.

wind energy: Energy obtained by using windmills to transform the kinetic energy of the wind into electricity. Wind energy is an indirect form of solar energy.

Notes

1. Aaron C. Kay and Steven Shepherd, "On the Perpetuation of Ignorance: System Dependence, System Justification, and the Motivated Avoidance of Sociopolitical Information," *Journal of Personality and Social Psychology* 102 (February 2012): 264–80.

2. Anthony Leiserowitz, "Communicating the Risks of Global Warming: American Risk Perceptions, Affective Images, and Interpretive Communities," in *Creating a Climate for Change: Communicating Climate Change and Facilitating Social Change,* ed. Susanne C. Moser and Lisa Dilling (New York: Cambridge University Press, 2007).

3. Albert Bandura, *Self-Efficacy: The Exercise of Control* (New York: W. H. Freeman, 1997).

4. Gary Braasch, *Earth Under Fire: How Global Warming Is Changing the World* (Berkeley: University of California Press, 2005).

5. Lynne Cherry and Gary Braasch, *How We Know What We Know About Our Changing Climate: Scientists and Kids Explore Global Warming* (Nevada City, CA: Dawn, 2008).

Index

Figures, graphs, and tables are indicated by *f*, *g*, or *t* following the page number.

EMPOWERING YOUNG VOICES FOR THE PLANET